José Vasconcelos

Also by Ilan Stavans

Fiction

The One-Handed Pianist
The Disappearance

Nonfiction

A Critic's Journey
Gabriel García Márquez: The Early Years
The Hispanic Condition
Art and Anger
The Riddle of Cantinflas
Imagining Columbus
The Inveterate Dreamer
Octavio Paz: A Meditation
Bandido
On Borrowed Words
Spanglish
¡Lotería! (with Teresa Villegas)
Dictionary Days
Resurrecting Hebrew

Anthologies

The Norton Anthology of Latino Literature
Tropical Synagogues
The Oxford Book of Latin American Essays
Becoming Americans: Four Centuries of Immigrant Writing
Growing Up Latino (with Harold Augenbraum)
Mutual Impressions
The Oxford Book of Jewish Stories
Wáchale!
The FSG Book of 20th-Century Latin American Poetry
The Scroll and the Cross
The Schocken Book of Modern Sephardic Literature
Lengua Fresca (with Harold Augenbraum)

Conversations
Love and Language (with Verónica Albin)
With All Thine Heart (with Mordecai Drache)
Eight Conversations (with Neal Sokol)
What Is la Hispanidad? (with Iván Jaksić)
Knowledge and Censorship (with Verónica Albin)
Conversations with Ilan Stavans

Cartoons
Latino USA (with Lalo Alcaráz)
Mr. Spic Goes to Washington (with Roberto Weil)

Translations
Sentimental Songs by Felipe Alfau

General
The Essential Ilan Stavans

Editions
The Collected Stories by Calvert Casey
The Poetry of Pablo Neruda
Collected Stories by Isaac Bashevis Singer (three volumes)
Encyclopedia Latina (four volumes)
Selected Writings by Rubén Darío
I Explain a Few Things by Pablo Neruda
Cesar Chavez: An Organizer's Tale
Spain, Take This Chalice from Me by César Vallejo

José Vasconcelos

The Prophet of Race

Ilan Stavans

Rutgers University Press

New Brunswick, New Jersey, and London

Library of Congress Cataloging-in-Publication Data

Stavans, Ilan.
  José Vasconcelos : the prophet of race / Ilan Stavans.
       p.   cm.
  Includes bibliographical references and index.
  Includes an English translation of Vasconcelos's "Mestizaje" from his
The cosmic race and his lecture "The race problem in Latin America," one
of three Harris Foundation lectures originally delivered at the University
of Chicago in 1926.
  ISBN 978-0-8135-5063-3 (hardcover : alk. paper) — ISBN 978-0-8135-
5064-0 (pbk. : alk. paper)
  1.   Vasconcelos, José, 1881–1959—Criticism and interpretation.
2. Vasconcelos, José, 1881–1959—Philosophy. 3. Vasconcelos, José,
1881–1959. Raza cósmica. 4. Mestizos. 5. Mestizaje. 6. Cosmology.
7. Latin America—Race relations. I. Vasconcelos, José, 1881–1959.
Raza cósmica. Mestizaje. English. II. Vasconcelos, José, 1881–1959. Race
problem in Latin America. III. Title.
  F1234.V3S73 2011
  305.80098—dc22

                                                        2010040717

             A British Cataloging-in-Publication record
         for this book is available from the British Library.

This volume copyright © 2011 by Rutgers, The State University

Preface, essay "The Prophet of Race," and scholarly apparatus copyright
© 2011 by Ilan Stavans

Translation of "Mestizaje" copyright © 2011 by John H. R. Polt

"The Race Problem in Latin America" reprinted, with minor alterations,
from José Vasconcelos and Manuel Gamio, *Aspects of Mexican
Civilization* (Chicago: University of Chicago Press, 1926), by permission
of the University of Chicago Press.

Visit our Web site: http://rutgerspress.rutgers.edu

Manufactured in the United States of America

. . . the *mestizo* will produce a civilization more universal in its tendency than any other race in the past.

—José Vasconcelos

Contents

Preface

José Vasconcelos's *La raza cósmica* (The Cosmic Race), a book explaining why *mestizos* are called to create a balanced, harmonious civilization that will dominate the world in the twenty-first century and beyond, remains enormously influential in the Spanish-speaking world as well as among Latinos in the United States. Since its original publication in 1925, it has been copiously debated by politicians and intellectuals alike.

Vasconcelos (1882–1959) was an educator and intellectual, Mexico's secretary of education, the first chancellor of the most important public institution of higher learning in Latin America, and also a candidate in the nation's 1929 presidential election. But he is mostly known as a thinker interested in a variety of topics, from the role of emotions in human life to the junction where race, science, and politics meet. Unfortunately, he is also recurrently portrayed as a fraud—*un charlatán*.

The accusation is not unfounded. Vasconcelos's central argument in *The Cosmic Race*, using social Darwinism as his platform, is pseudoscientific, not to say spurious. His diet of biological, anthropological, and sociological sources is bizarre. And, even more dangerous, his opinions, developed in reaction to British philosopher Herbert Spencer's views of racial purity and Austrian scientist Gregor Mendel's theory of transmitted hereditary, have a Nietzschean echo that suspiciously relates them to the misguided theories on the superiority of the Aryan race advanced by Adolf Hitler in Germany in the 1930s.

Actually, *The Cosmic Race* does not appear to be much read today, at least not in its entirety. People are only interested in the essay "Mestizaje," which constitutes about one-seventh of the book's content and, for better or worse, has become a surrogate not only for *The Cosmic Race* but for Vasconcelos's entire oeuvre. The essay served as prologue to the first edition and became the first chapter in the second edition of 1948. The rest of the book consists of impressionistic travel pieces on trips to Brazil, Uruguay, and Argentina, all of which appear to have been inserted as fillers.

Wanting to find an overall plan for Human History, which he conceives as written with capital letters, Vasconcelos argues that mixed marriages—racial miscegenation—result not in the detriment but in the improvement of society. "The *mestizo* and the Indian, and even the black," he writes, "surpass the white in count-less genuinely spiritual abilities." He adds: "The Hispanic race," which, after tracing the evolution of humankind Vasconcelos believes comes fifth as a racial group in the historical hierarchy, has ahead of it "this mission of discovering new zones of the spirit."

Vasconcelos was instrumental in the development of Mexico into a modern nation. That development was the result of his experiences in the United States, where he lived (Texas, California, and New York) during different periods of his life. His exposure to "Yankee ways," as he calls them, left a deep impression. In his four-installment memoirs, which he composed over a period of more than twenty years (in English, the autobiography was published in 1963 in an abridged translation called *A Mexican*

Ulysses), he discusses, often from an ethnic perspective, his journey from the outskirts of culture to center stage.

People have tried to ignore Vasconcelos's racial statements, which has not done much to eclipse them. He remains a vital reference, in part because of his love/hate relationship with Mexico. He was an inspiration for the student upheaval of the 1960s in Mexico that resulted in the Tlatelolco massacre of 1968. He also served as an ideological standard-bearer for the Chicano movement that began in that same decade, and for pan-Latino thinkers through the 1990s.

My purposes in the present volume are multiple. Vasconcelos remains an elusive intellectual reference, constantly mentioned but seldom read. For years the only available English translation of "Mestizaje" was by Didier T. Jaén, published in 1979 by the Department of Chicano Studies at California State University in Los Angeles. In 1997, Johns Hopkins University Press reprinted it in the book series Race in the Americas, edited by Robert Ried-Pharr. This version included an afterword by Joseba Gabilondo, a scholar specializing in Basque culture.

The rendition of "Mestizaje" by John H. R. Polt, emeritus professor of Spanish at the University of California, Berkeley, captures the essay's crispness, highlighting its raw, mystifying aspects. Accompanying Polt's translation is Vasconcelos's little-known lecture "The Race Problem in Latin America," written a year after *The Cosmic Race* appeared, where the author widens his scope on race in Mexico and, by extension, in the Spanish-speaking Americas. The lecture, one of three sponsored by the Norman Wait Harris Memorial Foundation, was delivered at the University of Chicago. Because Vasconcelos's audience was made up of English-language speakers, he reflected on the different racial relations that define the United States and Latin America.

It is important to advise readers that the narrative voice of "Mestizaje" and "The Problem of Race in Latin America" showcases itself as erudite. Vasconcelos parades an array of scientific, intellectual, and historical references that are both wide and heterogeneous. Although I offer footnotes to significant historical, intellectual, and scientific figures, my recommendation is to play Vasconcelos's game without being distracted.

These two pieces are accompanied by my profile "The Prophet of Race," in which I look in historical context at the polemist whom Octavio Paz, the Mexican poet and essayist and the winner of the Nobel Prize in Literature, called "an isolated monument that has not originated any school or movement," analyzing his life and status as a kind of Hispanic visionary who, while unread, commands substantial influence. (A chronology at the end of the volume provides a view of the full extent of his contribution.) By inviting readers to grapple with Vasconcelos's judgments, my hope is to contribute to the understanding of where his charisma as a Prophet of Race comes from and why "Mestizaje" has become a gospel.

José Vasconcelos

José Vasconcelos, 1914. *Photograph by Harris & Ewing. Library of Congress, Prints & Photographs Division.*

The Prophet

of Race

Ilan Stavans

Prophecy: The art and practice of selling one's
credibility for future delivery.
—Ambrose Bierce, *The Devil's Dictionary*

In a letter written in Madrid dated May
25, 1921, Alfonso Reyes, man of letters and author of the
classic *Vision of Anáhuac*, considered to be the dean of
Mexican intellectual life in the first half of the twentieth
century (Jorge Luis Borges described Reyes as "the most
accomplished stylist of the Spanish language"), gave
his friend and colleague José Vasconcelos some stinging
counsel. Reyes, whose lifelong impetus was to renew
Mexican culture from the pithy influence of positivism,
had met Vasconcelos almost a decade and a half earlier
as part of an intellectual movement in Mexico City that
came to be known as Ateneo de la Juventud (Athenaeum
of Youth). Thus, he was familiar with Vasconcelos's oeuvre
when he wrote:

I have to give you two bits of advice, because my experience as a reader dictates it to me: first, try being clearer when defining your philosophical ideas, as sometimes you offer an overwrought presentation. Place yourself outside your own purview, reading what you've just written objectively, not letting yourself be carried away or wrapped up with the course of your own thoughts. In order to write well, one must think with one's hands as well, not only with the head or heart. Second, place your ideas in successive order, not encrusting them on each other. Some of your paragraphs are confusing because in them you deal with totally different things, and the result is that they don't even appear to be serious.

Reyes's criticism is not unwarranted. Vasconcelos was a polymath, devoting himself from an early age to a vast number of pursuits, from politics to education, and from philosophy to the administration of cultural affairs. But he was mostly self-taught, and his rancorous, rambunctious spirit and his lack of a proper scholarly education resulted in a discombobulated body of work that, while substantial, is difficult to piece together. He was known throughout his life to shift gears in mid-argument, revoking most of what he had labored to establish up to that point. And even more worrisome was his penchant for revisiting his own opinions. For instance, having spent his early career celebrating Mexico as a generous land of enormous possibilities, after he lost the presidential election of 1929, which, he contended, was stolen away from him, he devoted the next decades to attacking his native country as unworthy, nearsighted, and treacherous. Reading Vasconcelos, as Reyes suggests, is an arduous task: the abyss between what he says and what he means is profound.

His influence is still palpable today, especially in the debate pertaining to racial theories, and far more in academic circles in the United States than in their counterparts in Latin America, including Mexico. As secretary of education, Vasconcelos was instrumental in building the educational system that allowed Mexico to become a modern nation. He sponsored "Los Tres Grandes," the legendary muralists Diego Rivera, José Clemente Orozco, and David Alfaro Siqueiros, in their double quest to bring art to the masses and infuse it with an ideological message that pushed for the reawakening of Mexico's mythical past. Vasconcelos was also the first chancellor of Mexico's Universidad Nacional, eventually known as Universidad Nacional Autónoma de México (U.N.A.M.), the country's largest, and Latin America's most preeminent, public institution of higher learning. In addition to these accomplishments, he produced a substantial body of writing: starting in 1907 with the book publication of his law school thesis, *Teoría dinámica del derecho* (Dynamic Theory of Law), and concluding, more than fifty years later, with the posthumous *Letanía del atardecer* (Afternoon Litany), published in 1959, he released approximately sixty books of essays, fiction, philosophical treatises, and history.

The cumulative effect is maddening. Not only does Vasconcelos repeat himself often, but he becomes his own detractor, critiquing his own views as unsubstantiated. His use of sources is unreliable. And his arguments are developed in an illogical, at times contradictory, fashion. Moreover, he promises what he cannot deliver. For instance, his four-volume *Obras completas* (Complete Works), released by Libreros Mexicanos Unidos between 1957 and 1961, are famously incomplete, in spite of having an accumulated length of several thousand pages, leaving out explosive pieces that Vasconcelos opted to eliminate.

This practice, of course, is not uncommon: authors are ambivalent about their own oeuvre, sometimes opting for self-censorship in the hope of apparent improvement. Then again, choosing the adjective *complete* in the title and delivering the opposite is a form of betrayal. Conversely, the *Breve historia de México* (Brief History of Mexico), published in 1938 at a length of 688 pages, is not brief. Nor is it a history of Mexico, as Vasconcelos, out of sheer fancy, denies attention to the pre-Columbian civilization that was essential in the making of the country.

Maybe his unsound scholarship is to be blamed for his limited readership, for Vasconcelos today has no followers. Still, a single one of his books, *La raza cósmica* (The Cosmic Race), subtitled *Misión de la raza iberoamericana. Notas de viaje a la América del Sur* (Mission of the Ibero-American Race. Travel Notes to South America), has acquired the status of a classic even though people do not read it. Proof of that absentee audience is the fact that the volume is unavailable in Spanish. In the English-speaking world, on the other hand, by virtue of this book alone—or better, as a result of its opening essay, "Mestizaje," which circulates like samizdat among activists—he is perceived as prophetic. A translation by Didier T. Jaén allowed its premise to serve as inspiration in marches and protests that fought for social justice, equality, and self-determination for minorities in the Southwest, in particular, Mexican Americans.

Indeed, his impact on Chicano activists, intellectuals, and political leaders looking for self-definition during the civil rights era was decisive. His canonization as a forecaster of things to come is based on his premise that *mestizos*, the crossbreed of Spaniards and the aboriginal population in Mexico and Central America during the colonial period, from 1519 to 1810, are slated to dominate the world. He calls this the Cosmic Race, and, interchangeably, the Brown

Race. The forecast served as a tool to make a diverse, heterogeneous Chicano constituency (farm workers, urban laborers, college students, housewives) coalesce as a political unit. Intriguingly, none of them appears to have read Vasconcelos in full (granted this is a nightmarish task), or at least to have tried to understand the extent to which "Mestizaje" is an essentialist text that lumps Mexicans, Central Americans, and Latin Americans into a single category without explaining their qualifying differences, as well as a polemical tract that excoriates blacks, Asians, whites, and other ethnic groups. (In later works, Vasconcelos, while condemning Nazism and its orchestration of the Holocaust, became an unrepentant anti-Semite.)

The civil rights era is not known for its subtleties. The struggle for self-definition overrode people's interest in differences. The use of stereotypes was rampant. And Vasconcelos's "Mestizaje" served as a conduit to ratify those stereotypes. A few decades earlier it had achieved the same effect in Mexico, when, after the revolution of 1910–1917, in which figures like Emiliano Zapata and Francisco "Pancho" Villa fought against a dictatorial regime that empowered Europeans at the expense of the natives, it championed the homogenization of Mexico as a *mestizo* nation without defining in clear terms what *mestizaje* meant. Clearly, Vasconcelos articulated in intellectual terms an ambiguous yet popular sentiment registered among the people in these crucial moments of Mexican history south and north of the Rio Grande: brown is power.

———

Vasconcelos is among the first to use the metaphor of the hyphen—in Spanish, *el guión*—to describe *mestizos*, an image that became ubiquitous at the end of the twentieth century. When describing the dilemma of identity of a Peruvian historian of the colonial period, "El Inca" Garcilaso de la Vega, he writes: "His mind, as his own blood, became then the hyphen, the meeting point of the Spanish-Indian tragedy, all of which through his genius he succeeded in transforming into a new broader concept of life." But before visiting Vasconcelos's peculiar understanding of brownness, it is important to define the term propelling his fame: *mestizo*. For it would be bogus to think that Vasconcelos made the word fashionable or that his ramblings gave it an original twist.

One learns little about the endless, mind-rattling permutations of the word from the simple, straightforward definition offered by the *Diccionario de la Lengua Española* (*DLE*), the official lexicographic arm of the Royal Academy of the Spanish Language, located in Madrid. The dictionary says that *mestizo* comes from advanced Latin, *mixticĭus*, meaning "mixed, juxtaposed" (*mixto*, *mezclado*), and not, as some linguists assume, from an aboriginal source. It then offers three definitions, which I hereby translate: "1. Said of a person born from parents of different races, especially a white man and an Indian woman, or an Indian man and a white woman. 2. Said of an animal or vegetable, resulting from two different races. 3. Said of a culture, of spiritual events, etc.: Coming from the mixture of different cultures." A few lines before, the *DLE* describes *mestizaje* as the crossbreeding of different races. But the dictionary ignores identity, a striking absence given that nowadays *mestizo* is a buzz term favored by millions in Mesoamerica from lower Mexico to Central America, a region that in pre-Columbian times included multifaceted cultures with shared agricultural, religious, technological, and economic lives.

But what are the uses of *mestizo*? Who is referred to by the term? How did the Mexican government invest in its meaning? What epistemological wars have surrounded that meaning? And how is the word understood in the United States, where it appears to have taken on a new life? People in Mesoamerica perceive themselves in ways that distinguish them from the rest of the hemisphere. Although African slaves were an important racial ingredient in the hodgepodge, the dominant groups are, as the *DLE* states it, the Iberian and indigenous. The conquest was a quick, successful military undertaking: Hernán Cortés arrived in Tenochtitlán, today's Mexico City, in 1519, with a couple of hundred men, and within a short time span, Spanish culture came to dominate, resulting in a hybrid civilization, part European and part Aztec, Mayan, Olmec, Toltec, and other variants.

Mestizo fills numerous spaces of meaning. In Spain, one hears the word used to describe, unflatteringly, what people call *sudacas*, immigrants from South America. The term is at the core of Mexican Spanish and is used in Mexico and by Mexicans far more than in any other national community, but it has other meanings, as when Filipinos use it for individuals who are of mixed indigenous Austronesian or other foreign ancestry. Often the term becomes a synecdoche to portray the Hispanic, Francophone, and Anglophone Americas. The hemisphere, one might say, is a miscellany. But isn't that a quality of the world entire, its jumbled nature, things having their place and time, with fusion as the beat? Is this region more of an assortment than the United States, for example? Terms competing with *mestizo* are also in vogue, from Puerto Rico's *jíbaro* to Ecuador's *ladino*, none of which mean the same thing. Actually, their connotations in history might be diametrically different. In any case, I have a Chinese-Cuban artist friend, and I am acquainted with a Peruvian politician from Cuzco who lives in Los Angeles, both of whom describe themselves as *mestizos*.

While the term might be synonymous with synthesis, it cannot be used indiscriminately. I recently learned, for instance, that *Harry Potter and the Half-Blood Prince*, the sixth installment of the saga, when translated into Spanish, was to be called *Harry Potter y el príncipe mestizo*. But the publisher thought one of the characters might be misunderstood to come from Mesoamerica, so the title was changed to *Harry Potter y el misterio del príncipe* (Harry Potter and the Mystery of the Prince). The word, hence, means amalgamation in a specific context: Latin America.

The word *mestizo* in sixteenth-century Spanish sometimes referred to children born out of wedlock, thus uniting it with the term *bastard*. In the colonial period, as the caste system was being established, to be a bastard signified that one's own genealogical stream was questionable. The Hispanic world caste system—with its elaborate taxonomy that included *españoles, criollos, mestizos, indios, mulatos, zambos,* and *negros*—emphasized purity of blood as proof of *casticismo,* authentic Iberian linage. For instance, Sor Juana Inés de la Cruz, a Mexican nun and unquestionably the best Spanish-language poet of the seventeenth century, born out of wedlock, probably needed to seek shelter in a convent in order to evade questions of legitimacy.

It took a long time for the idea of bastardy to metamorphose from a derogatory concept to one denoting alternative forms of pride, dignity, and self-respect. In 1810, when Miguel Hidalgo y Costilla and José María Morelos y Pavón, among other priests and activists in New Spain, launched the fight for Mexican independence from Spain, *mestizo* was in for a fresh start. There no longer was any shame in the fact that the majority of the country were by-products of Iberian and native miscegenation, from married and unmarried couples. A *mestizo* sensibility was at the core of the emergent national project. During the first battle in the war for freedom, Father Hidalgo y Costilla carried along a flag showing an image of the Virgin of Guadalupe, an icon closely linked to this sensibility. She is a Mexicanized Virgin Mary, a divine *mestiza* wearing a green tunic, surrounded by a halo and holding her hands together in prayer. Her image is ubiquitous nowadays, and the nation understands itself as *el pueblo guadalupano*, the Guadalupean people.

Mexico was the first country in Latin America to become autonomous, starting a domino effect that would continue well into the twentieth century. The independent government depicted the country's history as *mestizo*-driven. In the first half of that century, in the murals of Rivera, Orozco, and Siqueiros, *mestizaje* is the leitmotif: the past is depicted as a clash of civilizations, and the present as an attempt at balance. At that time, in part as a response to the spread of psychoanalysis, a debate among intellectuals ensued on the depth and complexity of the Mexican psyche. Aside from Vasconcelos, Samuel Ramos and Octavio Paz have participated, each to his own rhythm, with the ideological purpose of *mestizaje* at stake.

Samuel Ramos, in his 1934 volume *Profile of Man and Culture in Mexico*, looked at the *pelado*, the downtrodden *mestizo* making ends meet with a few pesos, as the emblem of the nation's soul. He studied his psychological traits and his relationship with authority (God, government, and *jefe*) to offer an ethnographic assessment. Octavio Paz, in his study *The Labyrinth of Solitude*, picked up where Ramos left off. In it Paz discusses, without the nod to Sigmund Freud that Ramos made, Mexico's attitude toward work, family, nature, and language. Ramos and Paz do not engage the term *mestizo* in the way Vasconcelos does. While they refer to it constantly, their collective portrait invokes it by employing other categories, for instance, *pachuco* in Paz's case, to describe Mexicans living in Los Angeles who have "become extremes of *la mexicanidad*," or Mexicanness.

———

The work of these intellectuals, Vasconcelos included, poses an unavoidable question that is crucial in understanding the kaleidoscope through which *mestizo* is observed. It has been the literary elite, mostly coming from the middle and upper classes, that has embraced the word as a valuable tool to understand politics and culture in Mexico and in other parts of the Americas. The people feel connected to the concept, but one hears it spoken more often among the educated than the common folks. *La raza*, "the race," is a figure of speech in street Mexican Spanish that refers to the masses. Other figures, not always easily translatable, are *el naco, la prole*, and *el pueblo*. Such alternatives suggest that, while Mexico does indeed perceive its foundation as *mestizo*, the malleable term is a construct exploited by the media and the government to give the nation, inside and out, a deliberate, easy-to-package sense of identity. This identity is then sold to tourists through movies, literature, museums, postcards, and other promotional material.

In popular culture, the Mexican psyche is best represented by several comedians. The foremost is Mario Moreno, best known as Cantinflas, whom Charlie Chaplin saw as his equivalent in the Spanish-speaking world. Cantinflas, in turn, saw Chaplin's tramp as his double in the English-language realm. The comparison is limited, because Chaplin's movies belonged to the silent era whereas Cantinflas's humor depended on his chaotic speech, which, among Spanish speakers, is recognized to this day as *el arte de cantinflear*, "the art of making sense out of nonsense." Moreno made dozens of movies that centered on Cantinflas—his *pelado*, to use Ramos's typology—a savvy, unemployed urban dweller who was always in trouble. Moreno himself was *mestizo*, as was Cantinflas, which accounts for the millions of people in the audience who adored him for the ingenuity with which he constantly looked disaster in the eye. Still, Cantinflas would describe himself in scene after scene as a happy-go-lucky fellow, never as a *mestizo*. Again, that identity was implied, not verbalized, in his adventures.

The second king of *mestizo* comedy was Tin-Tan, a darling of the *pachucada*, the Mexican American population in California, Texas, and other parts of the United States. Tin-Tan could not have cared less about the literary elite's reflections on *mestizaje*, yet he took Octavio Paz at his word, making "extreme Mexicanness" the target of laughter in numerous movies. In his parlance, he constantly used Spanglish, in itself a hybrid tongue. The third comic is Roberto Gómez Bolaños, known as Chespirito, a legendary actor who, as the Mexican film industry declined and the appeal of television soared, created an assortment of anti-heroes for the small screen, from El Chavo del Ocho, a small boy always playing with his neighbors on the patio of a lower-class housing project in Mexico City, to El Chapulín Colorado, a red cricket with superpowers who is always ready to help average people. And speaking of superheroes, there is Rodolfo Guzmán Huerta, who plays a *luchador*, a wrestler called El Santo. This serious wrestler, always wearing his signature silver mask, supports *la raza* against aliens, mad scientists, and corporate villains. All these are integral types of *mestizo* mythology, beloved in Mexico and throughout the Spanish-speaking world.

Intriguingly, the conversation on *mestizaje* has deep roots in the United States, where the Mexican American population exceeds thirty million and where the Mexican diaspora makes its base well beyond the Southwest, from rural areas to big cities. (One out of every four Mexicans lives north of the border.) *Mestizos* have left a mark in the United States since the Christian missions were established in Texas, California, and throughout the Pacific coast. The Treaty of Guadalupe Hidalgo in 1848, coming after the Mexican-American War, transferred large portions of territory from Mexico to the United States, along with the inhabitants in them. And the revolution led by Zapata and Villa, followed sometime later by the Bracero Program, increased the demographic presence of *mestizos* on the northern side of the divide.

Nevertheless, awareness of a *mestizo* sensibility did not take hold north of the Rio Grande, at least in public discourse, until the 1960s, when El Movimiento, the Chicano movement, emphasized a collective consciousness. The term *Chicano* itself, while etymologically distant from *mestizo*, is, in cultural terms, intimately linked to it: a Chicano then was a *mestizo* with a desire for freedom, autonomy, and maybe even self-rule. Activists linked the Virgin of Guadalupe, the mixed genealogical and cultural background, and a sense of ethnic pride with a *mestizo* identity that was crystallizing as a mechanism of self-determination.

Out of the Chicano movement came a theology, an educational approach that pushed for the opening of Chicano studies programs, a political alertness, and the conviction that *mestizaje* ought to be seen not only as a racial term but as unique perception of the self. As time went by, several thinkers reflected on that perception. Some were directly linked to El Movimiento, like Gloria Anzaldúa, whose 1987 feminist book, *Borderlands/La Frontera: The New Mestiza*, offered fresh insights into the adaptability of the term *mestiza*. For Anzaldúa, it meant to live defiantly, with the conviction that a hybrid life is perfectly suited for our changing times. Another English-language essayist attracted to the word is Richard Rodríguez. He has produced a trilogy of books, including *Brown: The Last Discovery of America*, in which he advocates that *mestizaje* is, actually, a most useful category to understand how the United States has become multicultural in recent decades.

The transformative power of the Latino minority, the largest and fastest-growing in the pluralistic United States, has had an effect on this debate. In colleges across the nation, the notion of *mestizaje* is part of the curriculum in Hispanic courses. A majority of Mexican Americans are *mestizos*, and Mexican Americans today are also recognized by the rubric *Latino*. Yet not all Latinos are Mexican American. On the one hand, the *mestizo* self pushes a portion of Mexican Americans to understand themselves as separate from other Latinos, although, as in the case of Anzaldúa, they make the concept of *mestizaje* permeable enough to serve them as a platform to relate to other people of color. On the other hand, there are some, including Rodríguez, who suggest that *mestizaje* is no longer a term defining an individual group alone. It has become universal. By virtue of the cross-fertilization defining the country in its entirety, we are all *mestizos* now, no matter if one comes from Bogotá, Beirut, or Jakarta. Shortly after his election in 2008, Barack Obama proudly called himself a "mutt," knowing that mongrels are all of us, in one way or another.

In short, the *DLE* might say that a *mestizo* is a person or culture born from different races, but it is something far bigger yet less tangible: a state of mind.

––––

Although Vasconcelos is an integral part of the cadre of Mexican intellectuals obsessed with the term *mestizo*, the concept remains frighteningly elusive in his oeuvre. "Mestizaje" refers to the ascendance of *mestizos* as the Cosmic Race. But he does not bother to explain who they are or where they come from. Nor does he appear to assume that these issues are already settled. What is unquestionable is his embrace of miscegenation. In his view, the mixing of races, rather than diminishing their individual qualities, emphasizes them. In Darwinian terms, juxtaposition is positive. He maintains that in other civilizations "reproduction has been accomplished in the manner of beasts, with no limit in quantity and no aspiration for improvement." Although Vasconcelos might have an incendiary argument, he is maddeningly obtuse in his presentation.

The 294-page first edition of *The Cosmic Race* was published in Barcelona by Agencia Mundial de Librería in 1925, when the author was forty-three. It was republished in Mexico City by Espasa-Calpe in 1948. In spite of the fact that in the interim Vasconcelos had changed his mind on a number of topics, other than moving "Mestizaje" from serving the function of prologue to becoming the first chapter, and adding a preface, the content is the same. In other words, no further explanation of *mestizo* is offered. Furthermore, in 1926 Vasconcelos published *Indología: Una interpretación de la cultura iberoamericana* (Indology: An Interpretation of Ibero-American Culture), where he reverses himself, implying that the indigenous population—for example, *el indio*, a social type about whom he nurtured ambivalent thoughts—played as important a role in the shaping of Latin America as *mestizos* did. (Vasconcelos uses the terms *Ibero-America* and *Hispanic America* synonymously.)

The abundance of references in "Mestizaje" makes for a bumpy read. Vasconcelos discusses Confucius, Plato's philosophy, Napoleon's military enterprise, the adventures of conquistadors like Hernán Cortés and Francisco Pizarro, the German geophysicist Alfred Lothar Wegener, the art of Spanish painters Diego Velázquez and Francisco Goya, the positivism of French thinker Auguste Comte, as well as mystical, scientific, and artistic traditions traced back to China, Egypt, and Greece. In the prologue to the 1948 edition (not included in this volume), he writes: "The central thesis of this book is that the various races of the earth tend to intermix at a gradually increasing pace, and eventually will give rise to a new human type, composed of selections from each of the races already in existence." Later he adds:

> Present world conditions favor the development of interracial sexual unions, a fact that lends unexpected support to the thesis that, for lack of a better name, I entitled: the future Cosmic Race. Nevertheless, it remains to be seen whether the unlimited and inevitable mixture is a favorable factor in the increment of culture or if, to the contrary, it will produce a decadence that now would no longer be of merely national but of worldwide proportions. This problem raises again the question the *mestizo* has often asked himself: Is my contribution to culture comparable to that of the relatively pure races that have made history up to our day, such as the Greeks, the Romans, or the Europeans? And, within each country, how do the periods of miscegenation compare with the periods of homogeneous racial creativity?

In "Mestizaje," Vasconcelos talks about the emergence of different racial groups and the attempts by previous civilizations to keep their racial components separate, for example, to resist racial intermingling. That is where Latin America stands alone, with an extraordinary opportunity for the future. A feature of the Hispanic world is its resistance to the elimination of difference. Unlike other civilizations that destroyed those in their midst who were different, in Latin America difference has been assimilated. "[T]hat gives us new rights and the hope of a historically unprecedented mission," Vasconcelos states. He points, as an example, to "the rigid line that separates black from white in the United States and the ever more rigorous laws that exclude the Japanese and Chinese from California."

He argues that "[e]ach of the great peoples of history has deemed itself the last and the chosen," adding that "[t]he Hebrews based their belief in their superiority on oracles and divine promises. The English base theirs on observations concerning domestic animals. Out of the observation of crossings and hereditary varieties of these animals grew Darwinism, first as a modest zoological theory, then as a social biology that assigns the Englishman absolute superiority over all other races. Every imperialism has need of a philosophy to justify it."

Vasconcelos's premises rely on, and are in opposition to, the thesis of English philosopher Herbert Spencer's Darwinian understanding of human evolution. Spencer used scientific data to indicate that individualization is the result of a slow process of evolution, which established the superiority of the white race and was accompanied by concepts applicable to societies advanced in their organization, like freedom and individual rights. In his understanding of human development, featured in *Principles of Biology* (1864), which he wrote after reading Darwin's *On the Origin of Species* (1859), he portrayed forms of social coalescence, from a military society that depends on force to keep its constituency in order, to one organized around industrial growth in which, as Spencer put it, the relationships between people is the glue keeping them together.

Vasconcelos bases his argument on Gregor Johann Mendel, whose series of genetic tenets—known as Mendelism—established the transmission of hereditary characteristics from organisms to their offspring. Another decisive influence was Friedrich Nietzsche, whose philosophy of morality, presented through aphorisms in *Human, All Too Human* (1878) and *Thus Spoke Zarathustra* (1883–1885), which the author of *The Cosmic Race* admired, was used by Adolf Hitler in Germany to justify the superiority of the Aryan race as the supreme ruler of the world. That philosophy of racial hierarchy led to state policies that resulted in the genocide of millions of so-called inferior people, including Jews and Gypsies.

The impact of Spencer and Nietzsche (the latter died in 1900, the former in 1903) in the early decades of the twentieth century was enormous. With the ideology of colonialism rapidly losing ground—Joseph Conrad's novella *Heart of Darkness*, with its portrait of how Europe's ventures in Africa could end in tragic disaster, was published in 1902, a year before Spencer's death—debates on racial hierarchies abounded. Although Vasconcelos was attracted to Spencer, he rejected the English thinker's belief in racial purity. He was, however, a by-product of Auguste Comte's positivism, a philosophy with a strong presence in Latin America at the end of the nineteenth century, which sought to modernize the region by emphasizing the role of reason in the shaping of human societies. Hence, Vasconcelos believed that a multidisciplinary approach to knowledge—history, psychology, anthropology, sociology, philosophy, and science—was needed to fully explain overall human change. But emotions, as Spinoza suggested in *The Ethics*, are at the forefront of human understanding. In the Hispanic world, raw emotions play an essential role in human interactions.

Positivism in Latin America was largely an ideology of modernization. Thinkers from Mexico to Argentina believed that awkward segments of society, like the indigenous population, needed to be educated in European mores, or else eliminated altogether, in order for everyone to taste the fruits of progress. Vasconcelos endorsed some of these ideas and refuted others. He perceived human evolution in the current stage as a struggle between England and Spain, between "Saxons and Latins," in which the latter, for the most part, have been the losers. The bulk of "Mestizaje" is devoted to explaining how a dramatic turn of events is under way, with the Latinos taking control of their own and the world's destiny. In other words, rather than thinking that Europe was the end of civilization, he trusted that it was only a stepping stone and that the colonials, at least those in the Americas, were called to supersede the imperial powers from the Old Continent in their vision.

According to Paz, "the work that Vasconcelos created has all the poetic coherency of the great philosophical systems, but not their rigor. It is an isolated monument and has not originated any school or movement." Paz is right: the philosophy of the author of *The Cosmic Race* is a personal creation, a set of grandiose statements that are at once ominous and incongruous. But that is not its worst quality: Vasconcelos attempted to develop a philosophy of race and ended up with a racist tirade. For in "Mestizaje" and "The Race Problem in Latin America" he vindicates *mestizos* at the expense of other groups, which he denigrates.

————

No matter how many readings of "Mestizaje" one attempts, the essay refuses to shed light on the global implications of *mestizaje*. Is Vasconcelos's argument really about *mestizos* being called to dominate the world, or is he talking about miscegenation as a general phenomenon? He answers the question by going back and forth between the two positions but never fully addressing the issue. However, in the prologue to the 1948 edition he seems to gravitate toward a less hopeful, more fatalistic stand than the one offered in the original edition of *The Cosmic Race*. He offers a few examples that show *mestizaje* as a major element in human history, regardless of race, epoch, or geographical location. Once again, these examples are muddled with gross assumptions, historical inaccuracies, and an abundance of stereotypes:

> Beginning with the most ancient race in history, the Egyptian, recent observations have demonstrated that Egyptian civilization advanced from the south to the north, from the Upper Nile to the Mediterranean. A predominantly white and relatively homogeneous race created a flourishing First Empire around Luxor. Wars and conquests weakened this empire and placed it at the mercy of black penetration, but the advance to the north was not interrupted. However, after a period of several centuries, the decadence of the culture was evident. It is presumable, then, that already by the time of the Second Empire, a new, *mestizo* race, with mixed characteristics of both the white and the black, had been produced. This is the race that brought about the Second Empire, more advanced and flourishing than the First. The period in which the pyramids were built, and the Egyptian civilization reached its summit, is the *mestizo* period.
>
> Greek historians are in agreement today that the Golden Age of Hellenic culture appeared as the result of a mixture of races. Here, however, the contrast between black and white was not present; it was

rather a mixture of light-colored races. Nonetheless, there was a mixture of races and cultural currents.

Greek civilization declines when the empire expands with Alexander, which facilitates the Roman conquest. Among Julius Caesar's troops, the new Roman mixture is already noticeable: Gallics, Spaniards, Britons, and even Germans, who collaborate in the feats of the Empire and transform Rome into a cosmopolitan center. It is a well-known fact that there were emperors of Hispanic-Roman blood. At any rate, the contrasts were not too violent, since the mixture was essentially of European races. The invasion by Barbarians who mix with native Gallic, Spaniards, Celts, or Tuscans, produced the European nationalities that have been the fountainhead of modern culture.

Vasconcelos then switches gears, reflecting on race in the New World. He hints that the United States is "nothing but a melting pot of European nations." He describes blacks as a segregated race forbidden to meld "yet the spiritual penetration they have accomplished through music, dance, and quite a few aspects of artistic sensibility has had great importance." And he adds: "After the United States, the nation with the most vigorous drive is the Argentine Republic, where the mixture of similar races, all of them of European origin, is again repeated. Here, Mediterranean types predominate, in contrast to the United States, where the Nordic types are predominant."

And then, in a sudden twist, Vasconcelos mocks *mestizos* in Mexico and Central America, suggesting that racial mixture of disparate elements might be noxious. He states, again absurdly, that Christianity eliminated cannibalism among the indigenous population of the Americas. And he belittles Asia for purportedly not embracing Christianity:

Thus, it can be readily stated that the mixture of similar races is productive, while the mixture of very distant types, as in the case of Spaniards and American Indians, has questionable results. The underdevelopment of the Hispanic American people, where the native element predominates, is difficult to explain, unless we go far back in time to the first example cited here of the Egyptian civilization. It so happens that the mixture of quite dissimilar elements takes a long time to mold. Among us, owing to the exclusion of Spaniards that was decreed after Independence, the mixing of the races was interrupted before the racial type was completely finished. In countries like Ecuador and Peru, political motives, as well as the poverty of the land, restrained Spanish immigration.

At any rate, the most optimistic conclusion that can be drawn from the facts here developed is that even the most contradictory racial mixtures can have beneficial results, as long as the spiritual factor contributes to raise them. In fact, the decline of Asiatic peoples can be attributed to their isolation, but also, and without a doubt, primarily, to the fact that they have not been Christianized. A religion such as Christianity made the American Indian advance, in a few centuries, from cannibalism to a relative degree of civilization.

Clearly, as Vasconcelos aged, his ideas on race and miscegenation evolved to the point that they became unintelligible. He was sour about his own place in Mexico's modern history, regretting lost opportunities. Yet in his mid-forties, when *The Cosmic Race* was first released, he appeared confident that hybridity in the Americas would allow the region to assume a key role in history. His belief was structured as a rejection of the United States as a nation that built itself on the premise of segregation.

This view is developed in a series of lectures he delivered in English at the University of Chicago in 1926, a year after *The Cosmic Race* was published, sponsored by the Norman Wait Harris Memorial Foundation, under the rubric "The Latin American Basis of Mexican Civilization." The lectures were released in book form, along with three others by Manuel Gamio, who at one point served as assistant secretary of education and was a distinguished scholar of indigenous affairs in his own right, as *Aspects of Mexican Civilization*, published by the University of Chicago Press.

The mandate of the foundation, in its own mission statement, was "the promotion of a better understanding on the part of American citizens of the other people of the world, thus establishing the basis of improved international relations and a more enlightened world-order." The statement added that "the aim shall always be to give accurate information, not to propagate opinions." This clearly is not the case with Vasconcelos's lectures. Titled "Similarity and Contrast," "Democracy in Latin America," and "The Race Problem in Latin America," they are not only intricate in structure, opaque in style, and simplistic in their overview of history; they also propagate Vasconcelos's dubious approach to social Darwinism, chiefly his notion that races appear and disappear in history according to a cyclical clock and that the ecosystem in which they exist justifies one of them overwhelming the others.

Above all, Vasconcelos's third and final Norman Wait Harris Memorial Foundation lecture is helpful in understanding his views on miscegenation. The first element one notices is the conundrum of its title: race in Latin America is a problem, which is an assertion not found in "Mestizaje." In the lecture, the line of reasoning in "Mestizaje" is distilled, making it somewhat easier for the reader to follow what Vasconcelos is eager to say. In fact, nowhere are his ideas on the *mestizo* more tangible than in "The Race Problem in Latin America." And nowhere are they more scathing either. The following passage is the closest Vasconcelos comes to sketching the features of the *mestizo*. He states that those features are commonly known, yet his portrait differs from those produced by writers who came before and after him, like Samuel Ramos and Octavio Paz, in that he presents the *mestizo* as a bon vivant, sharp in character yet psychologically unsound:

> The truth is then that whether we like it or not the *mestizo* is the dominant element in the Latin American continent. His characteristics have been pointed out many a time: a great vivacity of mind; quickness of understanding, and at the same time an unsteady temperament; not too much persistence in purpose; a somewhat defective will. It is curious to note that the blending of two different souls through inheritance has produced broader mental disposition. From a purely intellectual point of view I doubt whether there is a race with less prejudice, more ready to take almost any mental adventure, more subtle, and more varied than the *mestizo*, or half-breed. I find in these traits the hope that the *mestizo* will produce a civilization more universal in its tendency than any other race of the past. Whether it is owing to our temperament or to the fact that we do not possess a very strong national tradition, the truth is that our people are keen and are apt to understand and interpret the most contradictory human types. We feel the need of expressing life though many channels, through a thousand channels;

we are not addicted to local tradition or to the European, but we desire to know and to try all—the East and the West, the North and the South. A plurality of emotion, an almost mad desire to try and to live life from every point of view and every manner of sense experience—we are perhaps more truly universal than any other people. Notwithstanding, we sometimes appear to be bigoted and patriotically local, but this is a result of the dangerous political position in which we have been placed in recent years. On the other hand we are unstable, and this I believe can be easily understood by the biologist, as we are a new product, a new breed, not yet entirely shaped. I believe such weakness can be overcome by obtaining a clear definition of our aim and by devoting ourselves to a definite and a great task.

(An aside on the question of gender is appropriate here. It is imperative to notice that Vasconcelos looks at the world from an exclusively male perspective. Not only does he follow the Spanish syntax to describe his subject as *mestizo*, never *mestiza*, but his overall précis always stresses masculine qualities. He is, in part, a product of his time. For instance, when as minister of education he supported Los Tres Grandes, the three Mexican muralists, encouraging Frida Kahlo, Rivera's on-and-off life companion, who, granted, lived under his shadow, was never in Vasconcelos's agenda. He had no interest whatsoever in advancing women's art. Nor was he concerned with exploring sexual issues in his analysis of *mestizos*. Personally, he remained married to the same woman throughout most of his life, although, as a result of his constant traveling and consequent absence from home, the couple eventually separated.)

At any rate, Vasconcelos waits until the end of his description to present the *mestizo*'s worst qualities. He paints the *mestizo* as unable to understand himself and then suddenly praises the United States as a democratic model to emulate in racial terms. This troubling reversal of opinion is another example of the author's contradictory, self-defeating thought process:

> Many of our failings arise from the fact that we do not know exactly what we want. First of all, then, we ought to define our own culture and our own purposes, and educate ourselves to them. No nation has ever risen to true greatness without an ardent faith in some high ideal. Democracy and equal opportunities for every man has been the motto of the great American nation. Broadness, universality of sentiment and thought, in order to fulfill the mission of bringing together all the races of the earth and with the purpose of creating a new type of civilization, is, I believe, the ideal that would give us in Latin America strength and vision.

It is symptomatic that Vasconcelos almost always talks about *mestizos* as an archetype, seldom using the term to include himself—except in this passage, where he talks about what "we ought" to do (as Mexicans, ostensibly) in order to have a balanced identity. That is, here he is not only an observer; he is also the observed. He states that *mestizos* are still in an amorphous stage, not fully formed. Among his most significant statements is the programmatic "No nation has ever risen to true greatness without an ardent faith in some high ideal." Hence, he conceives of an education plan that will allow Mexico to flourish, although he is stunningly vague as to what that plan should look like and how it should be implemented. It presumably must enable the *mestizos'* worldview to be bold and universal in sentiment and thought so that they may take control of their own destiny.

———

I am certainly not the first to suspect that Vasconcelos deliberately confuses the concepts of race, nation, and civilization, at times talking about the three as if they were synonymous, while failing to relate them to the concept of class. I will not be the last either. For instance, throughout "The Race Problem in Latin America," he manifests ambivalence toward the United States, describing it as an example of the climax in the evolution of whites as a race. But he trusts that this supremacy is superficial. He argues that whereas the United States is a civilization that came into being when the Pilgrims, professing the Protestant faith, settled North America by "pushing the Indian back," in Mexico and elsewhere in Latin America, the Spaniards intermingled with the Indian population, creating a new breed that kept some of the European racial traits while incorporating others from Indian civilization.

The difference in approach, according to Vasconcelos, gave the United States a false feeling of superiority. Whites, in his view, lived isolated from the rest of the world. (Remember: his depictions were published in the 1920s, between the two world wars, a period known in the United States for its intense ethnic divisions.) He suggests that ostracizing minorities—blacks, Asians, Indians—will eventually backfire for the white majority, making it lose touch with the actual world and pushing it into a corner. Latin America, instead, had embraced, as he saw it, a more harmonious strategy, fostering diversity through hybridity. Although the region had not yet achieved its potential, the racial strategy inaugurated by the Spanish conquistadors during the conquest and in the colonial period will ultimately pay off when Mexico, and by and large Latin America, will superimpose themselves over other civilizations, including the United States.

This is because, as Vasconcelos announces in "Mestizage," since the middle of the nineteenth century, the leaders of Latin American independence "were concerned with freeing the slaves, declaring the equality of all men in natural law, the social and civic equality of whites, blacks, and Indians. At a critical moment in History, they formulated the transcendental mission that is assigned to our portion of the globe, the mission of ethnically and spiritually fusing all peoples." He recommends in "The Problem of Race" that "[i]f [the United States does] not wish to be overwhelmed by the wave of the Negro, of the Indian, or of the Asiatic, [it] shall have to see that the Negro, the Indian, and the Asiatic are raised to the higher standards of life, where reproduction becomes regulated and quality predominates over numbers." He reasons that when "the dominating race stands apart and takes no interest in the life of the inferior, the inferior tends instinctively to increase its numbers in order to compensate through numbers what the dominating race achieves through quality."

Vasconcelos's penchant for prophecy is tangible in the previous quotation: he envisions a time like the civil rights era when the ostracism of blacks and other ethnic groups was no longer sustainable. A struggle against oppression was launched that resulted in desegregation. But his prophetic view stops short of imagining a United States in which a black would preside from the White House. And even less feasible is a future in which a mongrel, as Barak Obama defined himself, would be elected by the popular vote.

Equally prophetic is his reflection on the limits of equality promulgated by the constitutions established in the nineteenth century from Mexico to Argentina. There is "a vital question in Latin America," he affirms in the preface to the 1948 edition of *The Cosmic Race*, "and one that is often debated is this: Should all the Latin American states remain loyal to their written constitutions dating from the beginning of the nineteenth century that establish the sovereignty of the people expressed by the vote, or is it better to look for more native standards such as military dictatorships in the name of the republic or in the name of socialism?"

Furthermore, Vasconcelos claims both in "Mestizaje" and in "The Race Problem in Latin America" that racial purity ought to be abandoned. As he states it in the lecture, "humanity is going back to Babel, and by this I mean that the day of the isolated civilization is over. In this new coming-together of all the races we ought not to repeat the methods of the past, the methods that transformed Babel into a curse. Babel became a curse because the different people did not understand each other and consequently, instead of concurring in a common purpose, they entered into competition and jealousy that destroyed every one of them."

———

Vasconcelos was an educator obsessed with spreading knowledge across society. This meant incorporating marginalized sectors, like the indigenous population, and, in equal measure, establishing a pedagogical system that valued science and the humanities and stressed the importance of libraries as centers for community engagement. In his view, the intellect was the motor behind modernity. Mexico, in his eyes, was a civilization that resulted from the encounter of two other civilizations: Spain and the aboriginal tribes of pre-Columbian times. There was creativity in that encounter, and there was fury. His contradictory feelings toward Mexico and the United States, toward *mestizos,* and toward himself, were the result of his upbringing. Vasconcelos himself was a half-breed, part Portuguese, part indigenous. (The surname was originally spelled Vasconcellos.) His experience growing up near the U.S.-Mexican border was a defining factor in his education, stressing otherness as an element of his character.

Born on February 28, 1882, in Oaxaca, the capital city of the Mexican state of the same name, he was five when his family moved to Piedras Negras, in the northern state of Coahuila. Living on the borderland was decisive for him: he would not only learn English (in 1888 he entered an English-language primary school in Eagle Pass, Texas), but on the street and in school he was exposed to the racial tension between Anglos and Mexicans, a factor that deeply shaped his worldview. In his autobiography, *A Mexican Ulysses,* he describes the ambivalence he felt. On one hand he loved studying and on the other he realized that knowledge is never achieved in a vacuum. Learning always depends on context. Vasconcelos's experience among Mexicans and Mexican Americans in Eagle Pass, who ought to be seen as precursors of those who participated in the Chicano movement, symbolized for him the crossroads where learning and self-respect meet. Here is a segment translated by W. Rex Crawford:

> School had been winning me over gradually. Now I
> would not have exchanged it for any pastime. I never
> missed a class. All things considered, the school was
> very permissive and the teachers fair. The year we had

a woman teacher I got my first punishment. I don't remember what I had done, but I was forced to hold up my hand. The blow I received was given with a will, but still without anger.

The fair-mindedness of the teachers stood out in connection with the arguments arising from Texas history. The independence of Texas and the war of 1847 divided the class into rival camps. We Mexicans in the class were not numerous, but we stood our ground. When I say Mexicans, I include the many who lived in Texas, and whose fathers had become naturalized, but who made common cause with us because of their descent. And if they had not, it would have turned out just the same, since the Yankees put us all in the same category. When it was said in class that a hundred Yankees could put to fight a thousand Mexicans, I got up and said, "That isn't so!" And it made me still more angry if some pupil compared the customs of the Mexicans to those of the Eskimos, and said, "Mexicans are semi-civilized people." At our house, on the other hand, we believed that Yankees had just recently acquired culture. I would get up in class and argue, "We had printing before you did." And the teacher would lecture me, "Yes, look at Joe: he's a Mexican. Isn't he civilized? Isn't he a gentleman?"

For the moment, this fair observation established a cordial relationship, but soon our passions were aroused again. We made a date for recess; blows were exchanged. The fight became a personal one. We went to the neighborhood field. A large group followed us. We began to fight in earnest. From the beginning, I got the worst of it. My opponent beat me up methodically. Next day, at lunch time, while I was brooding over my defeat of the previous day, a Mexican fellow student, one of those born and brought up beside the river, came up. "Here, take this," he said, handing me a sharp razor. "I'm lending it to you. The gringos are afraid of the blade. Keep it for this afternoon."

When we came out of school, my foe took up a position in front of his gang. I came closer, with my friends. I made him a sign, inviting him to fight, and at the same time showed the open blade in my right hand. "Not that way," said Jim, "the way we did yesterday." "No, not like yesterday," I said, "like this." My Mexican friend told me, "Now these gringos won't bother you." It was lucky that I managed to make myself respected in this way, for I loved the classes.

The use of terms like *Yankee* and *gringo* is part of Vasconcelos's rhetorical approach. In his opinion, Mexico did not define itself in isolation but vis-à-vis its neighbors. The language he uses to describe those neighbors is, in and of itself, a manifestation of that relationship based on the recognition of a deep, irreconcilable difference. As time went by, he developed a view of the United States based on tribalism, not integration, and defined by a Protestant ideal of self-development. This resulted in a *weltanschauung* that is forward-looking. Yet he also saw that race polarized the United States. He looked at the various racial groups that constituted it as units never amounting to a whole. Only the white majority had access to power. Blacks, Asians, Mexicans, and others lived in a subaltern state. Gringos and Mexicans in Texas, therefore, would not be able to find a common ground: while sharing the same space, they were doomed to live apart.

In 1895, the family relocated to Mexico City, where Vasconcelos attended middle school and high school, after which he studied law at the Escuela de Jurisprudencia, graduating in 1905 with a thesis called "Teoría dinámica del derecho" (A Dynamic Theory of Law). The thesis was published as a book in 1907, the same year that Vasconcelos, already a married man (he married Serafina Miranda, a native of Oaxaca, in Tlaxcala), was admitted to the bar. Subsequently, he worked as a secretary and as a law clerk. His early experience as a lawyer took place against the background of political turmoil. Dictator Porfirio Díaz, in power since 1878 (with an intermission of four years between 1880 and 1884), led the nation with a heavy hand. Like other young intellectuals of the period, Vasconcelos was an anti-Porfirista who believed the best route for Mexico was an orderly transition to democracy like the one in the United States.

The transition was far from peaceful. A revolution would sweep society in 1910, leaving an estimated one hundred thousand dead. A couple of years prior, on October 28, 1908, Vasconcelos, along with friends, had founded the anti–Porfirio Díaz literary salon called Ateneo de la Juventud. Soon after, he formally joined the Partido Nacional Antireeleccionista in Mexico City. Not only was he one of its leaders, but he become the codirector of its weekly periodical, *El Antireeleccionista*, soon suppressed by the Díaz police. When, in 1910, Vasconcelos published *Gabino Barreda y las ideas contemporáneas* (Gabino Barreda and Contemporary Ideas), about the physician and positivist thinker close to the regime, Díaz reached his limit and ordered Vasconcelos's arrest. To avoid imprisonment, he escaped to New York, where he stayed for three months.

———

Throughout this decade, a series of political alliances defined his path. Upon his return to Mexico City,

Vasconcelos backed Francisco I. Madero, who represented an alternative to Díaz and around whom the political opposition coalesced. Madero was a presidential candidate in the middle of a campaign when he was imprisoned, along with other Antireeleccionistas, in 1910, in San Luis Potosí. Released after his father posted a bond, Madero was smuggled into the United States. In San Antonio, he drafted a document called "Plan of San Luis Potosí," calling for annulment of the recent presidential election of Porfirio Díaz and proclaiming the need to orchestrate an uprising against the dictatorship, thus setting in motion the Mexican Revolution.

In retaliation, Díaz's police pursued Vasconcelos, forcing him to closes his law office and relocate once again, this time to Washington, D.C., where he continued working for Madero. In July 1911, after Díaz's resignation and Madero's triumph, he returned to Mexico City and reopened his office. He was named president of the Ateneo de la Juventud. Soon after, Madero changed the name of the Partido Nacional Antireeleccionista to the Partido Constitucional Progresista. Vasconcelos was made vice president of its executive committee.

The storm was only beginning, though. (In Vasconcelos's autobiography, the volume devoted to this period is titled "La tormenta" [The Storm].) One of Madero's supposed supporters, Victoriano Huerta, plotted against Madero. Huerta was named the country's president on February 18, 1913, and four days later Madero was assassinated, an event that Vasconcelos saw coming. In March of that year, Venustiano Carranza, a supporter of Madero, issued the "Plan of Guadalupe," repudiating Huerta. Sharing his ideological approach, Vasconcelos was sent to London and Paris as Carranza's confidential agent. It was Carranza who named him director of the Escuela Nacional

Preparatoria in 1914, beginning a career in education that would ultimately define him. His support for Carranza was short-lived, however, and he decided to resign his post. Shortly later he was jailed but escaped to Aguascalientes, where he befriended General Eulalio Gutiérrez, soon to be named Mexico's interim president.

Gutiérrez asked Vasconcelos to be his minister of public instruction. But more ideological skirmishes convinced him to withdraw from public life months later and Vasconcelos decided to devote his time to writing, publishing a series of books. He accepted a post with the Escuelas Internacionales, left for South America, then returned to New York, where he worked as a corporate lawyer; he then relocated to California, where more books followed. It was only after Carranza was killed, in 1920, that Vasconcelos returned to Mexico City, where he became the first chancellor (the term in Mexican Spanish is *rector*) of U.N.A.M., a post that inspired him to begin a formal campaign against illiteracy.

He traveled constantly in the country, promoting the school system, launching the publication of a series of classics in translation, starting a free breakfast program in Mexico's public schools, selling to people the philosophy behind the shield and motto for U.N.A.M.: "Por mi raza hablará el espíritu" (My Spirit Shall Speak in Behalf of My Race), and inaugurating the Primer Congreso Internacional de Estudiantes. The trajectory culminated on October 12, 1921—Columbus Day—when he was named secretary of education. He was a fan of Herbert Spencer's *Education: Intellectual, Moral, Physical* (1861), an attempt to look at the role of pedagogy from a plethora of perspectives, and emulated its conclusions. In *A Mexican Ulysses*, he states that his educational plan was simple and well organized—"simple in structure, but vast and complicated in its realization, a plan which managed to attack every problem":

In a word, my plan set up a Ministry with branches all over the country, divided functionally into three great Departments: Schools, Libraries, and Fine Arts. Under the heading Schools came all scientific and technical instruction in its various branches, theoretical as well as practical. The creation of a special Department of Libraries was a permanent necessity, for the country was struggling along without serving the reader, and only the State can create and maintain such services, which are complementary to the school, the adult school, and schools for youths who cannot matriculate in secondary or professional schools. The Department of Fine Arts took under its wing—starting with the teaching of singing, drawing, and physical education in all the schools—all the institutes for more advanced work in the arts, such as the old Academy of Fine Arts, the national Museum, and the Conservatories of Music. From the beginning in the primary schools the three Departments worked together, each charged with its proper function.

It is difficult to emphasize the importance of the U.N.A.M. motto: "Por mi raza hablará el espíritu" is as much an ideological slogan as it is Vasconcelos's own raison d'être. The spirit speaks for a race. And each race has its own unique spirit.

––––––

This understanding became apparent to him as he reflected on the role of the indigenous population in Mexico. In fact, he began to ponder the concept of *indigenismo*: an ideology that actively articulated what it was to be indigenous in modern Mexico. However, Vasconcelos did not use this ideology to give voice to that population. For most of his career, it was by means of the educated elite that *el indio* spoke to others.

At the time there were close to sixty-five different aboriginal languages in Mexico, from Otomí and Tarascan to Mazatec and Totonac. He supported schools sponsored by the Catholic Church to attack illiteracy among the Indian population and to teach them the Spanish language. "The Indian Department," he stated in his autobiography, "should have no other purpose than to prepare the native to enter the common school by giving him the fundamental tools in Spanish, since I proposed to go contrary to the North American Protestant practice of approaching the problem of teaching the native as something special and separate from the rest of the population."

"The Indian question," as it was referred to in the 1930s, is a theme present in Vasconcelos's career from *Indología* to about 1945. In "Mestizaje" he is intrigued by the indigenous population but only factors it in his views on miscegenation by suggesting that the Indian is the counterpart of the Spaniard. But in 1926, when "The Race Problem in Latin America" was delivered as a lecture, his opinions on the indigenous population, not only in Mexico, but throughout Latin America and in the United States, were stronger. He says, for instance, that the Indians, culturally speaking, are an empty civilization. He holds that "the Indian has no civilized standards upon which to fall back."

This simplistic approach makes Vasconcelos justify, in a backhanded fashion, their destruction by the New England settlers and, similarly, their surrender to the forces of the Spanish Empire. Left alone, he argues, the indigenous population in the New World might have ultimately perished on its own, without Europeans accelerating that process. In *A Mexican Ulysses* he develops these thoughts:

> The inspiration for teaching the Indians came to us, as
> was natural, from the Spanish tradition. It was because

it had denied and forgotten this tradition that the Republic had accomplished nothing in its century of independent life. The tradition also served to give us support against the system that had been permeating the teachers of Mexico, leading them to imitate the North American approach to the Indian problem. The system is founded on positivistic ethnography, which exaggerates racial differences and makes the savage a creature apart, a kind of link between the monkey and the man. Spanish educators from before the time of ethnology, as a result of insight that amounted to genius, and also as a result of experience, had, after a trial, abandoned the system of applying special methods to the Indians in separate schools. In place of segregation they set up a system of integration of the races in school and worship. From this fusion, the homogeneity of our people, the relative harmony of the races, has arisen. Protestantism on the other hand, with its scientific pretensions, both before and after my period of activity, has been setting up special schools for Indians and this can lead only to copying the North American plan, a plan for better division based on color and race. Adopting the North American system is therefore equivalent to undoing the most profound and effective work of the colony, the tight union of Indians and whites. The ethnological thesis which is implicit in the system of educating Indians and whites together is one that I expounded in my book, *La raza cósmica.*

As secretary of education, Vasconcelos also patronized a movement, led by muralists Rivera, Orozco, and Siqueiros, to use public art as a means of enlightenment. He supported the nation's folk arts, founding a national symphony, and carrying out the first census of indigenous regions and languages. He established the beginnings of the National Polytechnic Institute, developed "cultural missions" in rural towns, and was named Maestro de la Juventud (Teacher of Youth) by students in Colombia, Peru, and Panama.

This massive pedagogical effort reached its apex in 1924 when Vasconcelos, with dreams of leading Mexico as a whole, resigned as secretary of education, accepting the candidacy for the governorship of the state of Oaxaca, where he was popularly elected, although the central government, fearing his ideological nativism and, more concretely, his unpredictable behavior, refused to recognize him in office.

In 1928, Vasconcelos was nominated by the Partido Constitucional Progresista as its presidential candidate. Álvaro Obregón, who had previously been president from 1920 to 1924, won the election, but before he could begin his second term, he was assassinated. A year later Vasconcelos ran again, this time against Pascual Ortíz Rubio. He campaigned along Mexico's Pacific coast, then through the central and northern states. It was a controversial election. Vasconcelos had strong popular support but was opposed by both the United States and Mexico's central government, so he ended up exiled to the United States after issuing in Nogales his "Plan of Guaymas," advocating a Mexican rebellion. Disillusioned with political efforts, he left for Panama, where he lectured against American imperialism and the Calles regime. In subsequent years he published a book called *Ética* (Ethics), as well as a collection of short stories and a disquisition on Simón Bolívar and the Monroe Doctrine.

The rise of Hitler in Europe made Vasconcelos feel anxious. He had read Hitler's *Mein Kampf* and realized the impact of its message. Toward Hitler he felt contradictory feelings: admiration and fear. He perceived him less as a politician than as a symbol. Vasconcelos commented on this ambivalence approximately a year after World War II erupted. "Hitler, although he wields absolute power, finds himself a thousand leagues from Caesarism," he wrote in the essay "La inteligencia se impone" (Intelligence Prevails), published in 1940. "Power does not come to Hitler from the military base, but from the book that inspires the troops from the top. Hitler's power is not owed to the troops, nor the battalions, but to his own discussions. . . . Hitler represents, ultimately, an idea, the German idea, so often humiliated previously by French militarism and English perfidy. Truthfully, against Hitler we find civilian-governed 'democracies' fighting. But they are democracies in name only."

His defeat as a presidential candidate, the political trifles he engaged in with Carranza, and his sense that the ideals of the Revolution had been betrayed made him bitter. In *A Mexican Ulysses*, he describes the various regimes, from the late 1920s to the late 1930s, as "barbarous administrations." In an interview published shortly after his death, Vasconcelos, with the same regret he displayed in the 1948 prologue to *The Cosmic Race*, said that what the country had done, on the political stage, aroused in him "more nausea than admiration." The interviewer asked what he thought of the Mexican people. He replied: "They are a people made up overwhelmingly of cowards."

In recognition of his career, in 1946 he was named director of Mexico's Biblioteca Nacional. The position was ceremonial but had a clear purpose, because the regime in power, to the extent possible, wanted to keep Vasconcelos out of the political arena. The last decade of his life was marked by bitterness. He ranted frequently against Mexico's governing elite and issued melancholic statements on how Mexico had betrayed its own potential as a modern nation. He also catered to the notion of a posthumous life as a prophet, forecasting a future in which the United States would become subservient to Mexico. He had come to believe that both his itinerant life and the voluminous writings he was leaving behind would be seen by future generations as visionary. Mexico would one day revaluate its own physical, spiritual, and intellectual aptitudes. Latin America as a whole would come to play a defining role in geopolitics. And the United States, always bullying its neighbors, would be brought to its knees, not through war but by means of natural evolution.

———

At the time of his death, on June 30, 1959, in Mexico City, Vasconcelos's supporters were handily outnumbered by his detractors, an equation that defines his reputation since then. In *The Labyrinth of Solitude*, Paz makes the case that "[i]f the Revolution was a search and an immersion of ourselves in our own origins and being, no one embodied this fertile, desperate desire better than José Vasconcelos, the founder of modern education in Mexico." He adds: "His work was brief but fecund, and the essence of it is still alive. In part he carried on the task begun by Justo Sierra, which was to extend elementary education and to improve the quality of instruction on the higher levels, but he also tried to base education on certain principles that were implicit in our tradition but had been forgotten or ignored by the positivists."

Paz portrayed Vasconcelos as believing that the Revolution was going to rediscover the meaning of Mexican history. "The new education was to be founded on "our blood, our language and our people," he writes. In Paz's take, the character of the educational movement fostered by Vasconcelos was organic, and after the revolution that swept Mexico in 1910, Vasconcelos implemented it, in enthusiastic form, based on the principles pushing for a modernized version the struggle had promoted. Paz thought of him as an extraordinary man who was also a by-product of the Mexican Revolution. "Poets, painters, prose writers, teachers, architects and musicians all collaborated in the project," he argued. "All, that is, of the Mexican intelligentsia, or almost all. It was a social effort, but one that required the presence of a man who could catch fire and then transmit the enthusiasm to others. Vasconcelos, as a philosopher and a man of action, possessed that unity of vision which brings coherence to diverse plans, and although he sometimes overlooked details, he never lost himself in them. His work, subject to a number of necessary and not always happy corrections, was the work of a founder, not of a mere technician."

Intriguingly, Paz's view of Vasconcelos as an educator contains the element that makes him a prophet for the masses: his conviction that self-knowledge as well as collective knowledge brings forth change, and change is revelatory. "[He] conceived of instruction as active participation," Paz argues. His holistic portrait is linked to the notion that in the pursuit of knowledge, science and the arts are siblings:

> Schools were established, readers and the classics were published, and cultural missions were sent to the remotest part of the country. At the same time, the intelligentsia turned toward the people, discovering their true nature and eventually making them the center of its activities. The popular arts emerged again, after centuries of having been ignored; the

regional dances with their pure and timid movements, combining flight and immobility, fire and reserve, were danced for a wider audience. Contemporary Mexican painting was born. Some of our writers turned their eyes to the colonial past, and others used Indian themes; but the most courageous faced up to the present, and created the novel of the revolution. After the lies and pretences of the [Díaz] dictatorship, Mexico suddenly discovered herself, with astonished and loving eyes: "We are the prodigal sons of a homeland which we cannot even define but which we are beginning at last to observe. She is Castilian and Moorish, with Aztec makings."

The "prodigal sons," Mexico discovering "herself with astonished and loving eyes . . . Castilian and Moorish, with Aztec makings"—these haunting images evoke *mestizo* in its essence. Yet Vasconcelos is remembered less because of his educational ideas than as a result of his essentialist theory of the supremacy of the brown race. That supremacy comes from its capacity to find power in impurity. To mix is to reinvigorate, he contends.

The idea became exceptionally appealing to Mexican students in the 1960s, who themselves saw the governing Partido Revolucionario Institucional (PRI), in power since Vasconcelos had lost the presidential election in 1929, as a dictatorship that needed to be tumbled. The Cosmic Race—not the book, but the concept passionately presented in it—became a slogan. Brownness no longer had to be subservient. It was time to revolt. Vasconcelos's futurism was an inspiration.

Those who participated in the Chicano movement fought along the same lines. After centuries of subjugation, the awakening to a sense of uniqueness and possibility that took place during the civil rights era empowered them to recognize their role in history. There is no proof that leaders like Cesar Chavez, Dolores Huerta, and Reies López Tijerina read *The Cosmic Race*. Nor, it appears, did the lawyer and activist Oscar "Zeta" Acosta; Rodolfo "Corky" González, author of the poem "I Am Joaquín"; or *Los Angeles Times* journalist Rubén Salazar. Vasconcelos's endorsement of half-breedism was simply in the air.

He was a kind of Philip K. Dick, a paranoid transcendentalist who foreshadowed the rise of La Raza. In the chromatic spectrum of race in the 1960s, Chicanos were the hyphen, the in-between in the United States, neither white nor black but brown. Brownness, in their view, meant energy. Gloria Anzaldúa used the concept to embrace the idea that women of color were united at the core. Richard Rodríguez meditated on it as a way to understand the roots of a multiethnic America. Again, Vasconcelos's book was a classic, unread yet in the background, less as a manual for the revolution and more as gospel. The time for upheaval could wait no longer, for *The Cosmic Race* announced that purity of blood was on its way out and *mestizos* were leaders in a new world order.

Ironically, never does Vasconcelos ponder in "Mestizaje" or "The Race Problem in Latin America" the place of Latinos north of the Rio Grande (often referred to, in the early twentieth century, as "the Spanish-speaking people" or by their national ancestry, as Mexicans, Cubans, or Puerto Ricans, for example). His racial hierarchy includes whites, blacks, Asians, and Indians, but not Hispanics. In other words, he talks about *mestizaje* as a harbinger for change in Latin America, but he does not consider this population, which by the dawn of the twenty-first century would become the largest and fastest growing, as a catalyst for change inside the United States. As in the case of Paz's misrepresentation of Chicanos in the first chapter of *The Labyrinth of Solitude*, called "The *Pachuco* and Other Extremes," this might be another instance of Mexican intellectuals' nearsightedness concerning the Mexican diaspora living on the other side of the country's northern border.

In spite of this silence, it is worth asking, by way of conclusion: Will Vasconcelos's essentialist racial theory continue to play a role in the future among Mexican Americans and other Latinos, even though "Mestizaje" and his other writings remain unread? My guess is yes, as long as the feeling of alienation prevails and the struggle to bring justice and equality looks for idols in history that might give it traction.

Mestizaje

José Vasconcelos

Translated from
the Spanish by
John H. R. Polt

[I]

In the opinion of prominent geologists, America contains some of the most ancient regions of the world. The Andes are certainly made of material as old as any on our planet; and not only is the land ancient: the traces of life and of human culture are also of an age that exceeds all our calculations. The architectural ruins left by our fabled Mayas, Quechuas, and Toltecs are evidence of civilized life that precedes the oldest establishments of the peoples of Europe and the Orient. A growing body of research has come to support the view that Atlantis was the cradle of a civilization that flourished thousands of years ago in that lost continent and part of what is now America; and the notion of Atlantis evokes the memory of mysterious origins: the Hyperborean continent, lost but for the traces of life and culture that are occasionally found

45

beneath the snows of Greenland; the Lemurians, or black race of the south; the Atlantic civilization of the red man; the subsequent appearance of the yellow race; and, finally, the civilization of the whites. This legendary hypothesis, so profound, explains the course of human history better than do the learned speculations of geologists like Ameghino, who situate the origin of man in Patagonia, a land we know for sure to be of recent geological formation.[1] Wegener's theory of continental drift, on the other hand, according to which all the land masses of Earth were at one time united in a single continent that has been gradually breaking up, powerfully supports the notion of great prehistoric ethnic empires.[2] Without having to resort to the hypothesis of intercontinental migrations over lost land bridges, it allows one easily to imagine that in some specific part of a continuous land mass a race should have undergone the process of development and decline until it was replaced by another. It is also interesting to take note of an additional point at which ancient tradition coincides with the most recent geological findings: according to Wegener, the connection among Australia, India, and Madagascar was severed before the separation of South America from Africa, which confirms that the site of Lemurian civilization disappeared before the flourishing of Atlantis and that Atlantis was the last continent to be lost, since scientific research has shown that the Atlantic is the most recently formed ocean.

While the origin of this theory is more or less buried

---

1. Florentino Ameghino (1854–1911), Argentine naturalist, paleontologist, anthropologist, and zoologist.

2. Alfred Lothar Wegener (1880–1930), German geophysicist and meteorologist, proposed the theory of continental drift, suggesting that the continents shifted around on the earth's surface. Because of a lack of factual evidence, the theory was not accepted until the 1950s.

in a tradition as obscure as it is redolent, there survives the legend of a civilization born of our forests or spread to them after a period of mighty growth, whose traces are still to be seen at Chichén Itzá and Palenque and every other place shrouded in the lasting mystery of Atlantis—the mystery of the red men who, after dominating the world, caused the precepts of their wisdom to be engraved on the Emerald Tablet, some splendid Colombian emerald that, at the time of geological upheavals, was borne to Egypt, where Hermes Trismegistus and his followers learned and transmitted its secrets.[3]

If, then, we are ancient in terms of geology and also in terms of tradition, how can we continue to accept the newness that our European ancestors invented for a continent whose existence predates the formation of the land from which they set out in discovery and reconquest?

The question is enormously important for anyone intent on finding a plan in History. Those who see events only as an aimless chain of invariable repetitions might see little point in discovering the great age of our continent; and the works of contemporary civilization would scarcely arouse our interest if the palaces of the Toltecs had nothing to tell us but that civilizations follow one another, leaving behind them nothing but a few pieces of masonry, or a vaulted roof, or a ridged one. Why start all over, if four or five thousand years from now speculation about the ruins of our trivial contemporary architecture is to be nothing but a pastime for yet another race of newcomers? Scientific history, perplexed, leaves all these nagging questions unanswered. Empirical history, afflicted with myopia, bogs down in details but fails to identify even one predecessor

---

3. Hermes Trismegistus, representation of a syncretism between the Greek god Hermes and the Egyptian god Thoth.

of historical times. It shuns general conclusions and sweeping hypotheses; but it falls into such puerilities as cranial indices and the description of utensils, along with many another merely external detail, trivial except when integrated in a sweeping, comprehensive theory.

Only a spiritual leap, sustained by facts, will bring us to a vision that transcends the micro-ideology of the specialist. From that position we can probe the mass of events to find in them a direction, a rhythm, and an aim. And precisely where the analyst finds nothing, the synthesis and the creator find light.

Let us therefore attempt to form explanations, and to do so not with the imagination of the novelist, but with intuition based on the facts of history and science.

The race we have agreed to call Atlantic rose and fell in America. After an extraordinary flowering, its cycle and particular mission completed, it sank into silence and progressive decay until it was reduced to the petty empires of the Aztecs and the Incas, wholly unworthy of the superior earlier culture. With the decline of the Atlantic race, the dynamic process of civilization shifted to other places and other breeds: it dazzled in Egypt; it gained breadth in India and in Greece as it took root in new races. The Aryan, mingling with the Dravidian, produced the people of Hindustan, while creating Hellenic culture through other mixtures. The foundations of Western or European civilization were laid in Greece, and this white civilization expanded until it reached the forgotten shores of America to consummate a labor of recivilization and repopulation. And so we have four periods and four human lineages: the black, the red, the yellow, and the white. The last of these, after a formative period in Europe, has invaded the whole world and come to believe in its mission of dominance, just as each earlier dominant race believed in turn. The supremacy of the whites will of course also be temporary, but their mission differs from that of their predecessors: their mission is to serve as a bridge. Throughout the world the white man has created the conditions for the fusing of all races and cultures. The civilization achieved by him and shaped by our age has established the material and spiritual bases for the union of all men in a fifth race, a universal race that is the fruit of all earlier races and surmounts all that is past.

White culture is expansive, but it was not Europe as a whole that was charged with initiating the reincorporation of the red world into the forms of that not yet universal culture represented during centuries of domination by the white race. This transcendental mission was reserved for the two boldest branches of the European family, the two strongest and most dissimilar human types: the Spaniard and the Englishman.

Ever since the beginning, from the time of the discovery and conquest, it was Spaniards and Englishmen— or Latins and Saxons if we wish to include the Portuguese and the Dutch, respectively—who accomplished the task of beginning a new period of History by conquering and peopling the new hemisphere. They may have thought of themselves merely as colonizers, as transplanters of culture, but they were in fact laying the bases of a period of general and definitive transformation. The so-called Latins, bold and brilliant, seized the best regions, those they thought richest, and the English had to settle for the leftovers of fitter peoples. Neither Spain nor Portugal allowed the Saxon to approach her dominions, certainly not with arms, and not even to participate in trade. Latin superiority was indisputable at the outset. No one could have suspected, in those times of the papal bull that divided the New World between Portugal and Spain, that a few centuries later the New World would no longer be Portuguese or Spanish, but English. No one could have imagined that the humble settlers along the Hudson and the Delaware, peaceful and hardworking, would step by step gain possession of the biggest and best stretches of land until they had established the republic that is today one of the greatest empires in History.

Our time has become, and continues to be, a struggle of Latin against Saxon, a struggle of institutions, aims, and ideals, a crisis in the centuries-old struggle that begins with the destruction of the Invincible Armada and intensifies with the defeat at Trafalgar. After that, however, the arena of combat begins to shift, to move to the new continent, where further disastrous incidents occurred. The defeats at Santiago de Cuba, Cavite Bay, and Manila are distant but logical echoes of the catastrophes that befell the Armada and the fleet at Trafalgar. And now the conflict is staged wholly in the New World. In history, a century is like a day; it is not surprising that we have not yet shaken off the impression of defeat. We go through periods of discouragement, we continue to lose not only territorial sovereignty but also moral authority. Far from feeling united in the face of disaster, our will is fragmented in pursuit of vain and petty goals. Defeat has brought us confusion of values and of concepts; the diplomacy of the winners deceives us after having defeated us; trade conquers us with its petty benefits. Stripped of our former greatness, we take pride in an exclusively national patriotism and do not even notice the dangers that threaten our race as a whole. We deny and reject each other. Defeat has degraded us to the point where we unwittingly collaborate in the enemy's policy of beating us piecemeal, of offering separate advantages to each of our brothers while sacrificing the vital interests of another. Not only in battle did they beat us; they continue to defeat us ideologically. The greatest battle was lost the day that each of the Hispanic republics set out to live on its own, detached from its sisters, negotiating treaties and receiving false benefits with no thought for the common interests of our race. Without knowing it, the creators of our nationalism were the best allies of the Saxon, our rival for the possession of the continent. The display of our twenty flags at the Pan-American Union in Washington is something we should see as mockery by astute enemies. Nonetheless, each of us takes pride in his humble rag, which represents an empty illusion, and our disunion in the face of the powerful North American Union does not bring forth even a blush. We do not notice the contrast between Saxon unity and the anarchy and isolation of Ibero-America's escutcheons. We maintain a jealous independence one of the other, but in one way or the other we submit to or ally ourselves with the Saxon Union. Even the unification of the five Central American peoples has remained unattainable, because an outsider has refused to sanction it and because we lack the true patriotism that is prepared to sacrifice the present to the future. A lack of creative thought and an excess of critical zeal, which, to be sure, we have borrowed from other cultures, draw us into fruitless arguments in which we no sooner affirm the oneness of our aspirations than we deny it; but we fail to notice that when the time for action comes, and in spite of all the doubts harbored by learned Englishmen, the Englishman seeks to ally himself with his brothers in America and Australia, and at that point the Yankee feels himself to be as English as is the Englishman in England. We shall never be great as long as the Spaniard in America does not feel himself to be as Spanish as are the sons of Spain. That does not prevent our being different whenever necessary, though never at the expense of our supreme joint mission. This is how we must proceed if Iberian culture is finally to yield all its fruits, if we are to keep Saxon culture from triumphing in America unopposed. It is useless to dream of any other solution. A civilization can be neither improvised nor cut off, nor can it be based on the paper of a constitution; it always grows in the course of centuries through a slow elaboration and distillation of elements transmitted and blended since the beginnings of History. That is why it is so foolish to date our patriotic sentiments from Father Hidalgo's call for independence, or from the Quito conspiracy, or from the great deeds of Bolívar.[4] If we do not root them in Cuauhtémoc and in Atahualpa, they will lack a solid foundation, though at the same time we must trace them back to their Hispanic source and shape them in keeping with what we should have learned from the defeats, which are also our defeats, of the Invincible Armada and Trafalgar.[5] If our patriotism is not linked to the different stages in the ancient struggle between Latins and Saxons, we shall never be able to bring it to the point at which it is more than a mere regionalism devoid of universal aims, and we shall see it inevitably degenerate into narrowness and parochial shortsightedness and the powerless inertia of the mollusk clinging to its rock.

Lest we be forced some day to renounce even our

4. Miguel Hidalgo y Costilla, aka Miguel Gregorio Antonio Ignacio Hidalgo y Costilla y Gallaga Mondarte Villaseñor (1753–1811), a priest and leader in Mexico's War of Independence from Spain. Simón José Antonio de la Santísima Trinidad Bolívar y Palacios, aka Simón Bolívar (1783–1830), Venezuelan military figure and the most important leader in South America's struggle for independence from Spain.

5. Cuauhtémoc, aka Cuauhtemotzin, Guatimozin, or Guatemoc (ca. 1502–1525), last Aztec ruler of Tenochtitlán, from 1520 to 1521. Atahualpa, aka Atahuallpa, Atabalipa, and Atawallpa (1497–1533), last ruler of the Inca Empire.

country, we must live in keeping with the superior interests of our race, even if these still fall short of the highest interests of humanity. The heart will evidently settle for nothing less than total internationalism; yet under the present circumstances of the world, internationalism would serve but to consummate the triumph of the most powerful nations, serve only the interests of the English. Even the Russians, with their population of two hundred million, have had to defer their theoretical internationalism in order to come to the aid of oppressed nationalisms like those of India and Egypt. At the same time they have reinforced their own nationalism as a defense against a disintegration that could only favor the great imperialist states. It would be childish, then, for weak peoples like ours to set about renouncing their singularity in the name of objectives unattainable in the real world. The present state of civilization still requires our patriotism as the guardian of our material and spiritual interests, but it is essential that this patriotism pursue great and transcendental aims. Its mission was, in a sense, cut short at the time of our independence, and now we must channel it once more toward its world-historical destiny.

The first stage of this basic conflict was fought in Europe, and we lost. Afterward, in the New World, where Spain's dominance gave us every advantage, Napoleonic stupidity caused Louisiana to be handed to the overseas English, the Yankees, thereby deciding the fate of the New World in favor of the Saxons. That "military genius" could not see beyond the miserable border disputes of the petty states of Europe and did not realize that the Latin cause, which he claimed to represent, was lost on the very day he was proclaimed Emperor, simply because that act placed the common destiny in the hands of an incompetent. In addition, European prejudices obscured the fact that the conflict whose significance Napoleon could not even imagine was already engaged on a universal scale in America. Napoleonic obtuseness was unable to suspect that it was in the New World that the destiny of Europe's races would be decided; and when it unthinkingly destroyed French power in America, it also weakened the Spaniards, betrayed us, and placed us under the sway of our common enemy. Without Napoleon, the United States would not exist as a world empire, and Louisiana, still French, would have to be a part of the Latin American Confederation. The effects of Trafalgar would in that case have been frustrated. No one so much as thought of any of this, because the destiny of the race was in the hands of a fool, because Caesarism is the scourge of the Latin race.

Napoleon's betrayal of the universal destiny of France also dealt a mortal blow to the Spanish empire in America at the moment of its greatest weakness. The speakers of English took Louisiana without a fight, saving their weapons of war for the now easy conquest of Texas and California. Without their base on the Mississippi, the Yankees, which is simply another term for the English, would not have been able to gain possession of the Pacific and would not today be the masters of the continent; they would have amounted to no more than a kind of Holland transplanted to America, and the New World would be Spanish and French. It was Bonaparte who made it Saxon.

Of course it is not only external causes—treaties, war, and politics—that decide the destiny of peoples. A Napoleon is nothing but the visible sign of vanity and corruption. There are times when the decline of mores, the loss of a people's liberties, and generalized ignorance have the effect of paralyzing the energy of a whole race.

The Spaniards went to the New World with the plethora of vigor that their successful reconquest of the Iberian Peninsula had left idle. Those free men called Cortés and

Pizarro and Alvarado and Belalcázar were neither lackeys nor Caesars, but great captains who combined a destructive impulse with creative genius.[6] On the morrow of victory they laid out new cities and drew up the laws that were to govern them. Later, when bitter disputes arose with the homeland, they knew how to repay tit for tat, as did one of the Pizarros during a famous trial. They all felt themselves to be the equals of the king, as El Cid had done, as did the great writers of the Golden Age, and as do all free men in great epochs of history.

But with the completion of the conquest, control over the entire new structure slipped into the hands of courtiers and royal favorites, men incapable, not only of conquering, but even of defending what others had conquered with their skill and daring. Degenerate sycophants capable of oppressing and humiliating the natives, but obsequious to royal power, they and their masters did nothing but degrade what the Spanish spirit had accomplished in America. The astonishing achievement begun by indomitable conquerors and consummated by wise and selfless missionaries sank toward collapse. A succession of foreign monarchs, so pitilessly portrayed by Velázquez and Goya in the company of dwarfs, buffoons, and courtiers, consummated the downfall of the colonial regime.[7] The obsession with imitating the Roman Empire—which has brought such harm to Spain as well as to Italy and France—militarism, and absolutism brought about decadence at the very time when our rivals, strengthened by virtue, grew and expanded in liberty.

---

6. Hernán Cortés (1485–1547), Spanish conquistador, credited with bringing down the Aztec Empire. Francisco Pizarro y González (ca, 1471–1541), Spanish conquistador, instrumental in bringing down the Inca Empire. Pedro de Alvarado (ca. 1485–1541), Spanish conquistador and governor of Guatemala. Sebastián de Belalcázar (ca. 1479–1551), Spanish conquistador of present-day Ecuador.

7. Diego Rodríguez de Silva y Velázquez (1599–1660), Spanish painter in the court of King Philip IV. Francisco José de Goya y Lucientes (1746–1828), Spanish painter and printmaker, considered one of the first modern artists.

Their sense of the practical, their instinctively successful strategies, developed along with their material strength. The colonists in New England and Virginia broke with England, but only so as better to grow and become stronger. Their political separation has never kept them from being of one mind and acting in unison in what concerns their common ethnic mission. Emancipation, instead of weakening this great race, split it into two branches, increased it, and, starting from the impressive nucleus of one of the greatest empires of all time, extended its power over the whole world. And ever since then, whatever is not conquered by the Englishman of the Old World is seized and held by the Englishman of the New.

On the other hand, we Spaniards, whether Spanish by blood or by culture, began to reject our traditions as soon as we achieved emancipation; we broke with our past, and there were those who disowned their blood, saying it would have been better had the conquest of our part of the world been carried out by the English—treasonable words, which some would excuse as a reaction against tyranny and as blindness born of defeat. Yet for a race to allow its fate to strip it of its historical sense is absurd, is equivalent to our denying strong and wise parents when it is we, not they, who are to blame for our decadence.

At any rate, the campaign to de-Hispanize us and the corresponding Anglification shrewdly promoted by the English themselves have clouded our judgment from the outset, making us forget that the humiliation of Trafalgar affected us, too. The presence of English officers on the staffs of the leaders of our wars for independence would have been the ultimate dishonor, had not the insult energized our proud old blood, which punished the pirates of Albion whenever they approached with rapacious intent. At such moments, the rebellious spirit of our ancestors responded with the voice of our cannons, at Buenos Aires as at Veracruz, at Havana, or at Campeche and Panama, each time that the English corsair would attack, disguised as a pirate to avoid responsibility in case of failure and sure of an honored place in the ranks of British nobility in case he triumphed.

In spite of this solidarity in the face of an invading enemy, our struggle for independence was diminished by provincialism and by the lack of vast and visionary plans. The race that had dreamed of ruling the world, the supposed descendants of Roman glory, yielded to the puerile satisfaction of creating mini-nations and petty principalities inhabited by souls that in every mountain range saw not a peak but a wall. With the illustrious exception of Bolívar and Sucre and the Haitian Pétion, and at most half a dozen more, the founders of our independence dreamt of Balkan glories.[8] Obsessed with the local and enmeshed in confused, pseudorevolutionary phraseology, they concerned themselves only with diminishing a conflict that could have been the start of a continent's awakening. To divide, to break up the dream of a great Latin power, seemed to be the aim of certain well-meaning but ignorant collaborators in the great work of independence, who deserve a place of honor within that movement but who could not and would not listen to Bolívar's inspired advice.

Of course in the case of every social process we must take into account the underlying causes that inevitably condition each particular stage. Our geography, for example, was and still is an obstacle to unity; but if we are to overcome that obstacle we shall first have to bring order

8. Antonio José de Sucre y Alcalá (1795–1830), Venezuelan independence leader, one of Simón Bolívar's closest friends and collaborators. Alexandre Sabès Pétion (1770–1818), founding father of Haiti and its president from 1806 until his death.

to our spirit by determining our goals and clarifying our ideas. Until we rectify our concepts we shall be unable to make our physical surroundings serve our purpose.

In Mexico, for example, almost no one except Mina thought of the interests of the whole continent; what is worse, for a whole century the prevailing patriotism taught that we triumphed over Spain thanks to the indomitable valor of our soldiers, with hardly a mention of the Cortes de Cádiz or the uprising against Napoleon, which electri-fied the whole race, or of the triumphs and sufferings of our Spanish American brothers.[9] This sin, which we share with all the other countries in America, is the product of a time when History is written to flatter despots, when jingoism, not content to depict its heroes as parts of a continentwide movement, presents them in isolation, without realizing that by so doing it diminishes them instead of aggrandizing them.

Another reason for these aberrations is that the native element had not, and still has not, wholly amalgamated with the Spanish blood; but this conflict is more apparent than real. Speak to the most exalted partisan of the Indians of the need to adapt ourselves to Latin culture, and he will not demur in the least; tell him that our culture is Spanish, and he will immediately raise objections. The stain of blood once shed remains, a cursed stain that centuries have not wiped away but that our common danger must remove. And there is no other way. Even the pure-blooded Indians are Hispanized, Latinized, just as our cultural environment is Latinized. Say what you will, the red men, the illustrious men of Atlantis from whom the Indian descends, went to sleep thousands of years ago,

---

9. Francisco Javier Mina (1789–1817), Spanish lawyer and army officer who fought in Mexico's War of Independence. The Cortes de Cádiz were a series of legislative sessions during the French occupation of Spain that served as an important step toward the nation's embrace of liberalism and democracy.

never again to awake. In History nothing returns, because History is transformation and renewal. No race returns; each one defines its mission, fulfills it, and departs. This truth is as valid for biblical times as for our own; it has been formulated by all the historians of antiquity. The days of the pure white race, today's conquerors, are as numbered as were those of its predecessors. By fulfilling its destiny through the technological development of the world, it has unwittingly laid the foundations of a new age, the age of the fusion and amalgam of all peoples. The Indian has no door toward the future but the door of modern culture, no path but the already cleared path of Latin civilization. The white man, too, will have to surrender his pride, and he will seek progress and ultimate redemption in the souls of his brothers of other races, and he will be absorbed and perfected in each of the higher varieties of our species, in each of the manifestations through which revelation becomes manifold and spirit more powerful.

———

In the pursuit of our ethnic mission, the war for independence from Spain was a dangerous crisis. By this I do not mean to say that it should not have been fought or won. There are times when ultimate aims must be put off; the race waits while the fatherland impels, and the fatherland is the immediate and imperative present. It was not possible to continue in dependence on a scepter that from blunder to blunder and calamity to disgrace had been steadily sinking until it fell into the ignominious hands of a Ferdinand VII.[10] Negotiations seeking to establish a free Hispanic federation would have been possible in the Cortes de Cádiz, but the only suitable response to the monarchy was to defeat its emissaries. On this point Mina

———

10. Ferdinand VII (1784–1833), king of Spain in 1808 and from 1813 to 1833.

saw clearly: first establish freedom in the New World, then overthrow the monarchy in Spain. Because the stupidity of the time kept this brilliant plan from being carried out, let us at least try to bear it in mind. Let us recognize that it was our misfortune not to proceed as cohesively as did the northerners, the remarkable race on which we like to heap insults simply because it has beaten us at each step of our centuries-old struggle. It triumphs because to its practical gifts it joins an intuitive knowledge of a clear historical mission, while we lose our way in a labyrinth of verbal will-o'-the-wisps. God himself seems to be guiding the steps of the Saxons, while we kill each other over questions of dogma or proclaim our atheism. How those potent builders of empire must be laughing at our Latin strutting and vanity! Their minds are not burdened with the Ciceronian weight of phraseology, nor is their blood riven by the contradictory instincts of a mixture of different races; but they committed the sin of destroying those races, while we assimilated them, and that gives us new rights and the hope of a historically unprecedented mission.

This is why our unfortunate stumbling steps do not induce us to give up; we vaguely sense that they will help us find our course. And we are right: it is in differences that we find the way. If we only imitate, we lose; if we discover, if we create, we shall triumph. Our tradition has the advantage of being more open to the outsider. This implies that our civilization, with all its faults, can be the one chosen to assimilate and refashion all men, and that within it the basis for a new humanity, its rich and varied plasma, is thus taking form.

This imperative of History first became manifest in the abundance of love that allowed the Spaniards to create a new race in combination with the Indian and the African, disseminating white stock by means of the soldier who engendered a native family, and Western culture by means of the teaching and example of the missionaries that made the Indian capable of entering the new stage, the stage of One World. Spanish colonization created a mixed race; this distinguishes its character, determines its responsibility, and defines its future. The Englishman continued to breed only with whites and exterminated the native, and he goes on exterminating him in the silent economic struggle that is more efficient than armed conquest. This proves how limited he is and indicates his decadence. On a large scale, it is the equivalent of the incestuous marriages of the Pharaohs, which undermined the vigor of that race; and it contradicts the ultimate aim of History, which is to achieve a fusion of all peoples and all cultures. Making the whole world English, wiping out the red man so that all of America may replicate a northern Europe made up of pure-blooded whites, is merely to repeat the victorious process followed by every conquering race. The red men did the same, and every strong and homogeneous race has done or tried to do the same; but this is no solution to the problem of humanity, and it was not for so petty a purpose that America was held in reserve for five thousand years. Our new-and-old continent is meant for something far more important: it is predestined to become the cradle of a fifth race that will combine all peoples to replace the other four that have independently been shaping History. It is on the soil of America that dispersion will come to an end; it is there that unity will be consummated by the triumph of fruitful love and that every separate lineage will be transcended. And in this fashion a synthesis will be engendered, a human type that shall combine all the treasures of History to give expression to the sum of the world's aspirations.

The Latin peoples, as we call them, having been most faithful to their divine mission in America, are those destined to consummate this synthesis. And that faithfulness to the hidden design is the guarantee of our triumph.

Even in the chaotic period of the struggle for independence, which deserves so much rebuke, one can glimpse that passion for universality that heralds the desire to blend all humanity in a universal synthesis. In part because he realized the danger into which we were falling as we split into isolated nations, and thanks also to his gift of prophecy, Bolívar already had formulated a plan for an Ibero-American federation that some fools oppose even now. And if the other leaders in that struggle generally had no clear concept of the future, if it is true that under the sway of provincialism, which we now call patriotism, or of limitation, which is now termed national sovereignty, each of them concerned himself only with the immediate fate of his own people, it is also surprising to note that almost all of them felt stirred by a universal human sentiment that corresponds to the destiny that we assign to the Ibero-American continent today. Hidalgo, Morelos, Bolívar, the Haitian Pétion, the Argentineans at Tucumán, Sucre—all of them were concerned with freeing the slaves, declaring the equality of all men in natural law, the social and civic equality of whites, blacks, and Indians.[11] At a critical moment in History, they formulated the transcendental mission that is assigned to our portion of the globe, the mission of ethnically and spiritually fusing all peoples.

Something was thus done among the Latins that never entered anyone's mind on the Saxon continent. There the opposite thesis continued to prevail, the open or tacit aim of cleansing the earth of red, yellow, and black men for

---

11. José María Morelos y Pavón (1765–1815), priest and revolutionary leader during Mexico's War of Independence.

the greater glory and happiness of the white. In fact, the two systems that to this day place the two civilizations in opposite sociological camps became clearly defined at that time. One seeks the exclusive supremacy of the white man; the other is creating a new race, a race of synthesis, which aims to embrace and express all humanity through a process of constant elevation. If proof were needed, it would suffice to observe the accelerating spontaneous intermixture among all peoples on the Latin continent and, on the other hand, the rigid line that separates black from white in the United States and the ever-more rigorous laws that exclude the Japanese and Chinese from California.

The so-called Latins—perhaps because, to begin with, they are not, properly speaking, Latins but a conglomerate of types and races—persist in not paying much attention to the ethnic factor in their sexual relations. Whatever opinions may be voiced in this respect, and no matter what repugnance prejudice may evoke in us, the fact is that there has been and continues to be a mingling of blood lines; and it is in this fusion of blood lines that we must seek the most basic distinguishing trait of the Ibero-American character. Economic competition may sometimes oblige us, and in effect has already obliged us, to close our doors to an inordinate deluge of Orientals, as do the Saxons. But in so doing, we proceed from reasons of a purely economic order; we recognize it to be unjust that peoples like the Chinese, which under the pious guidance of Confucian morality multiply like rabbits, should come to depress standards of living just as we are beginning to understand that intelligence can rein in and regulate our base animal instincts, which contradict a truly religious concept of life. If we reject such peoples, it is because as man progresses, his rate of reproduction decreases and he feels a horror of quantity, precisely because he has come to esteem quality. In the United States they reject Asiatics out of the same fear of being physically overwhelmed, characteristic of superior species, but also because they dislike the Asiatic, because they look down on him and would be incapable of interbreeding with him. The young ladies of San Francisco have refused to dance with officers of the Japanese navy, who are as well groomed, intelligent, and, in their way, as handsome as those of any other navy in the world. Nevertheless, these ladies will never understand that a Japanese can be handsome. Nor is it easy to convince the Saxon that if the yellow race and the black have their characteristic odor, so does the white man for others, even if we are unaware of it. In Latin America the revulsion felt by one blood on encountering another also exists, but in infinitely more attenuated form. There we find countless bridges toward the sincere and cordial fusion of all races. The contrast between the northerners' ethnic immurement and the southerners' far more relaxed openness is for us the most important as well as most favorable fact if one thinks, no matter how superficially, of the future, because it will then be immediately plain that we belong to tomorrow, while they are on the way to belonging to yesterday. The Yankees will create the last great empire of a single race, the final empire of white power, while we continue to suffer amid the vast chaos of an as yet inchoate breed. The germ of every human type will ferment within us, but we shall know that a better race is coming. Nature will not repeat one of its partial attempts in Spanish America: the race that will now issue from forgotten Atlantis will no longer be of a single color and particular features, will not be a fifth race or a sixth, destined to triumph over its predecessors; what will arise there is the definitive race, the integral race, the synthesis, made of the character and blood of all peoples and for that very reason better capable of true brotherhood and a truly universal vision.

To work toward fulfillment of this aim we must gradually create the cell tissue, as it were, which is to serve as the frame and flesh of the new biological entity; and in order to create this protean, malleable, profound, ethereal, and essential tissue, the Ibero-American race will have to comprehend its mission and embrace it as a form of mysticism.

Perhaps nothing is useless in the processes of History; even our physical isolation and our mistake in creating separate nations have kept us, as did the original fusion of blood, from incurring the Saxons' limiting defect of forming castes based on racial purity. History shows that such a process of rigorous selection, when carried on for a prolonged time, yields a physically refined breed, interesting but lacking vigor, beautiful in a strange way, like the ancient Brahmin caste, but, when it comes down to it, decadent. Never has such a breed exceeded other men in intelligence, virtue, or vigor. The road on which we have set out is far more daring; it breaks with ancient prejudices and would almost be inexplicable were it not founded on a kind of outcry reaching us from a remote distance—not the distance of the past but the mysterious distance whence come the presages of the future.

If Latin America were nothing but another Spain, to the same degree that the United States is another England, the old struggle between the two breeds would only be repeating its various phases on a larger stage, and one of the two rivals would eventually prove the stronger and would prevail. But this is not the natural law of opposites, neither in mechanics nor in life. Clash and struggle, especially when transported to the realm of the spirit, serve better to define the opponents, to impel each of them to the zenith of his destiny, and, in the end, to combine them in a common and victorious transcendence.

The Saxon's mission has been fulfilled earlier than has ours, because it was a more immediate mission and one already familiar to History; fulfilling it required nothing but following the example of other victorious peoples. The white man's values reached their peak, their bearers acting as a mere prolongation of Europe in that part of the American continent occupied by them. This is why the history of North America is like the uninterrupted and vigorous *allegro* of a triumphal march.

How different are the sounds that accompany the molding of Ibero-America! They resemble the profound *scherzo* of a deep and infinite symphony, voices that bear echoes of Atlantis, abysses dwelling within the eyes of the red man, who thousands of years ago knew so much and seems now to have forgotten everything. His soul is like a Mayan cistern in the middle of the forest, filled with deep, green, motionless water, so ancient that even the legend of its existence has been lost. And this stillness of the infinite is stirred up by the drop contributed to our blood by the black man, craving sensual delight, drunk with dancing and unbridled lusts. The yellow man appears, too, with the mystery of his slanted eye, which sees everything from a strange angle, which discovers who knows what new folds and dimensions. The mind of the white man, clear like his skin and his dreams, also plays its part. Hidden in the blood of Spain since the days of the cruel expulsion, strands of Jewish blood are revealed, and so are the melancholy moods of the Arab, the aftertaste of the morbid sensuality of the Muslim. Who does not hold some part of all this within himself, or does not want to hold it all? And then there is the Hindu, who will also come, who has already come in spirit; and though he is the last to come, he seems our closest kin. So many who have come, and others yet to come; and thus shall our heart grow sensitive and broad, reaching out to everything, holding everything, vibrating in sympathy with everything, but also bursting with vigor, laying down new laws for the world. And we sense that our head, too, will be different, making use of every perspective to achieve the marvel of transcending our globe.

[II]

After examining the long- and short-term potential of the mixed race that inhabits the Ibero-American continent and the destiny that is impelling it to be the first example of racial synthesis on our globe, we must consider whether the physical environment in which this breed is developing is suited to the aims set out for it by its biological attributes. The expanse already at its disposal is enormous; there is certainly no problem of space. The fact that its coasts offer few first-class harbors has almost no importance in view of the ever-greater progress in engineering. On the other hand, the basic necessities are undoubtedly more plentiful here than anywhere else on earth: natural resources, fertile arable land, water, and a favorable climate. Of course some will raise an objection with regard to this last factor: the climate, they will say, is hostile to the new race, because most of the available land lies in the hottest region of the globe. That, however, is precisely the advantage and the secret of the race's future. The great civilizations of the past arose in the tropics, and the final civilization will return to the tropics. The new race will begin to fulfill its destiny as new methods are invented to combat the adverse effects of heat on man while leaving intact all its beneficent capacity for the generation of life.

The triumph of the white man began with the conquest of snow and cold. The basis of white civilization is fuel. First it served as a defense during the long winters; subsequently men noticed that it contained a force that could be utilized not only for protection but also for work. At that point the motor was born, and thus all the technology that is transforming the world proceeds from the hearth and the stove. An invention of this sort would have been impossible in torrid Egypt and, as a matter of fact, did not occur there, even though that race was infinitely superior to the English race in intellectual capacity. For proof of this affirmation one needs only to compare the sublime metaphysics of the Egyptian priests' *Book of the Dead* with the banalities of Spencerian Darwinism.[12] Another thousand years of training and evolution would not suffice for those dolichocephalic blonds to bridge the abyss that separates Spencer from Hermes Trismegistus.

On the other hand, the Egyptians never dreamt of anything like the English ship, that marvelous machine derived from the Vikings of the North. The harsh struggle against his environment obliged the white man to devote his talents to the conquest of physical nature, and precisely this is his contribution to the civilization of the future. The white man taught dominion over matter. Some day white science will reverse the methods it employed to achieve mastery over fire and will make use of condensed snow, or electrochemical currents, or subtly magical gases, to destroy flies and other pests, to eliminate torpor and fever. Then all humanity will pour into the tropics, and in the solemn immensity of its landscapes the souls of men will achieve their plenitude. At first, the whites will try to

---

12. After Herbert Spencer (1820–1903), British philosopher, sociologist, psychologist, and political scientist, author of *A System of Synthetic Philosophy* and *The Man versus the State*, among other books.

use their inventions for their own benefit, but as science is no longer esoteric, they are unlikely to succeed in this. They will be overwhelmed by the avalanche of all the other peoples, and finally, swallowing their pride, they will join with the others to compose the new racial synthesis, the future fifth race.

The conquest of the tropics will transform every aspect of life. Architecture will abandon the pointed arch, the vault, and in general, roofs, which meet the need for shelter. The pyramid will once more be developed; men will build colonnades as gratuitous displays of beauty, and perhaps spiral constructions, because the new aesthetic will try to adapt itself to the endless curve of the spiral, which represents untrammeled aspiration, the triumph of being in the conquest of the infinite. The landscape full of colors and rhythms will convey its richness through emotions; reality will resemble fantasy. The aesthetic of cloudy skies and grays will be seen as a sickly art of the past. A polished and intense civilization will respond to the splendors of a Nature bursting with potency, arrayed in abundance, gleaming with light. The panorama of today's Rio de Janeiro or of Santos, with the city and its bay, can give us an inkling of what to expect as the future seat of the coming consummate race.

Once science has conquered the tropics, there will be a time when all mankind will settle in the planet's torrid zone. The Promised Land will then be the region that today includes all of Brazil, in addition to Colombia, Venezuela, Ecuador, part of Peru, part of Bolivia, and the northern part of Argentina.

There is the danger that science might outpace the ethnic process, so that the invasion of the tropics would occur before the fifth race is fully formed. If this should occur, there will be battles for the possession of the Amazon that will decide the destiny of the world and the fate of the definitive race. If the Amazon falls under the control of the English, who, whether European or American, are champions of a pure white race, then the appearance of the fifth race will be blocked. Such an outcome, however, would be absurd: History does not deviate from its path, and the English themselves, in the new climate, would become malleable, would become *mestizos*, though with them the process of integration and transcendence would be slower. The Amazon must therefore be Brazilian, Iberian, along with the Orinoco and the Magdalena. The resources of this zone, the world's richest in terms of treasures of all kinds, will allow the new racial synthesis to consolidate its culture. The world of the future will belong to whoever conquers Amazonia. Near the great river, Universopolis will rise, from which the evangelizers, the fleets and airplanes spreading the good news, will set out. If the Amazon became English, the capital of the world would not be called Universopolis but Anglotown, and fleets of warships would set out from there to impose on other continents the stern law of the supremacy of the blond-haired white man and the extermination of his dark rivals. On the other hand, if the fifth race gains control of the axis of the world of the future, airplanes and armies will spread out over the entire planet educating all peoples to achieve wisdom. Life based on love will come to express itself in forms of beauty.

Naturally, the fifth race will not attempt to exclude whites, any more than it intends to exclude any other people; it is constituted precisely on the principle of utilizing every potential to produce a more integrated power. Our aim is not war against the white man, but war against every sort of violent supremacy, whether of the white man or, conceivably, of the yellow man, if Japan should become an intercontinental threat. As for the white and his culture, the fifth race counts on them and still expects to benefit from their genius. Latin America owes what it is to the white European and will not disavow him; it owes a great part of its railways and bridges and business enterprises to the North American, and it similarly has need of every other race. Nevertheless, we accept the white man's higher ideals, not his arrogance; we wish to offer him, as to all peoples, a free fatherland in which he will find home and refuge, but not a prolongation of his conquests. The whites themselves, disturbed by the materialism and social injustice into which their race, the fourth race, has fallen, will come to us to aid in the conquest of liberty.

Perhaps the characteristics of the white man will predominate among those of the fifth race, but this supremacy must result from the free play of inclinations and not from violence or economic pressure. Superior cultural and natural traits will have to triumph, but this triumph will be solid only if based on its voluntary acceptance by the rational mind and on the unfettered choice of the imagination. Until now, life has been shaped by man's inferior faculties; the fifth race will be the fruit of his highest faculties. The fifth race is not exclusive: it garners life; hence the exclusion of the Yankee, like the exclusion of any other human type, would constitute an a priori mutilation, even more disastrous than a subsequent amputation. If we do not wish to exclude even those races that might be deemed inferior, it would be an even greater folly to banish from our enterprise a race possessed of energy and solid social virtues.

After explaining the theory of the formation of the future Ibero-American race and the way in which it will be able to utilize the environment in which it lives, we need consider only the third factor of the transformation that is taking place in the new continent, the spiritual factor that is to guide and consummate this extraordinary enterprise. Some may think that the fusion of today's different races into a new race completing and transcending all others will be a repulsive process of anarchic mongrelization, in comparison with which the English practice of marrying only within the same breed will appear as an ideal of refinement and purity. The first Aryans of India essayed precisely this English system to defend themselves against mixture with the colored races; but because the wisdom possessed by these dark races was the necessary complement to that of the blond invaders, the genuine culture of India only appeared after the centuries had consummated the mixture in spite of all written prohibitions. This predestined mixture, moreover, was useful not only for cultural reasons, but because man needs to draw physical renewal from the genetic pool of mankind. The North Americans hold very firmly to their resolution to maintain the purity of their breed; but this is because what faces them is the black man, the other extreme, as it were, the very opposite of a fungible element. In Ibero-America the problem does not arise in such stark terms; we have very few blacks, and most of them have already been turning into a population of mulattoes. The Indian is a good bridge toward fusion. Besides, the hot climate favors relations among all peoples and their unification. Furthermore—and this is essential—interbreeding among the races will not be owing to simple propinquity, as occurred at the beginning, when the white settler would take a native or black woman because no other was available. Eventually, as social conditions improve, crossbreeding will become ever more spontaneous, until it is no longer subject to necessity but to taste or even to curiosity.[13] Spiritual considerations will thus come to outweigh physical needs; and spiritual considerations should not be understood to mean thought, but rather the taste that is our guide in the mysterious choice of one person among so many.

[III]

This law of taste as the criterion for human relations is one that we have expounded more than once, calling it the law of the three stages of society, stages defined not in the manner of Comte but in a far more ample sense.[14] The three stages identified by this law are the material or military, the intellectual or political, and the spiritual or aesthetic. They constitute a process that is gradually liberating us from the rule of necessity and subjecting all of life to the higher criteria of feeling and imagination.

Material factors are the sole arbiters of the first stage; when peoples come into contact, they fight or combine in obedience only to violence and their relative strength. Sometimes one will exterminate the other, or they will form pacts in keeping with their needs and interests. The hordes or tribes of every race live like this. Under these conditions, physical force, the only cohesive element of the group, is also what causes one stock to mix with another. There can be no choice when the strong takes or rejects the conquered female as his whim may dictate.

---

13. *Translator's note*: Here and in subsequent passages, I render the Spanish word *gusto* as "taste." This, I believe, is its primary meaning in this context; but the reader should bear in mind that *gusto* can also mean "pleasure," a meaning that resonates to some degree in Vasconcelos's prose.

14. Referring to Auguste Comte (1798–1857), French philosopher and the founder of the doctrine of Positivism.

Of course the instinctive affinities that attract or repel in keeping with the mystery we call taste, the secret foundation of all aesthetics, underlie human relations even in this period; but the promptings of taste do not dominate in the first period, nor do they in the second, which is subject to the rigid norms of reason. Reason is also present in the first period as the motive of human conduct and action, but it is a weak reason, comparable to the suppressed taste. It is not reason that decides, but force, usually a brutal force to which judgment, enslaved to primitive will, submits. When judgment is thus perverted to become astuteness, it degenerates in the service of injustice. In the first period it is impossible to work for the harmonious fusion of the races, both because the rule of violence to which it is subject makes spontaneous cohesion impossible, and because geographical conditions do not even permit constant communication among all the peoples of the planet.

Reason tends to prevail in the second period, artfully utilizing the conquests of force and rectifying its errors. Borders are defined by treaty, and mores are organized according to the laws of mutual benefit and logic. Roman society is the most perfect model of this rational social system, although it actually began before Rome and still lingers in our age of nationalities. Under such a regime, the mixture of races arises in part from the whims of free instinct operating beneath the constraints of social norms, but especially from concern for immediate ethical or political benefits. In the name of morality, for example, almost indissoluble matrimonial bonds are imposed on persons who do not love each other; in the name of politics, inner and outer liberty is curtailed; in the name of religion, which ought to function as sublime inspiration, dogma and tyranny are imposed; but each case is justified with the appeal to reason, recognized as supreme arbiter of human affairs. A superficial logic and a questionable science are also the guides of those who condemn miscegenation in the name of a eugenics based on incomplete and false scientific data and therefore unable to produce valid results. This second period is characterized by faith in the formula; therefore in every respect it merely establishes norms for intelligence, limits for action, borders for the fatherland, and curbs to feeling. The rule, the norm, and tyranny are the law of the second period, in which we are today trapped and from which we must escape.

In the third period, whose coming can already be discerned in countless ways, our behavior will be guided not by poor reason, which explains but does not discover, but by creative feelings and irresistible beauty. Norms will be derived from the supreme faculty, the imagination; that is, men will live without norms, in a state in which all that is born of feeling is right. Instead of rules, constant inspiration. The worth of an action will not be sought in its immediate tangible results, as occurs in the first period, or in its obedience to certain rules of pure reason; even the ethical imperative will be transcended, and beyond good and evil, in the world of aesthetic emotion, the only concern will be that an action produce happiness through its beauty. To follow our impulse, not our duty; to walk the path of taste, not that of appetite or syllogism; to experience joy founded on love—that is the third stage.

We are unfortunately so imperfect that in order to achieve so godlike a form of life we shall first have to travel every road: the road of duty, where the lower appetites are purified and overcome; the road of dreams, which stimulates the highest aspirations. Then passion will come, redeeming us from low sensuality. To live passionately, to feel so intense an emotion toward all things that their movement falls into the rhythms of happiness—this is one aspect of the third period. It is achieved by releasing our divine impulse, so that with a single agile bound, without bridges of morality or logic, it may reach the zone of revelation. Unmediated intuition, which leaps over the chains of syllogistic reasoning and, being a passion, transcends duty from the outset and replaces it with exalted love, is an artistic gift. We know that both duty and logic are the scaffolding and mechanics of the building, but the soul of architecture is a rhythm that goes beyond the mechanical and obeys no law but the mystery of divine beauty.

What role is assigned in this process to that sinew of human destinies, the will, which the fourth race came to deify in the intoxicating moment of its triumph? The will is force, blind force that pursues confused ends. In the first period it is guided by the appetite, which uses it to satisfy all its whims; next the light of reason dawns, and the will is restrained by duty and shaped by logical thought. In the third period the will becomes free, transcends the finite, bursts and plunges into a kind of infinite reality, is filled with distant echoes and aims. No longer satisfied with logic, it puts on the wings of imagination, descends into the deepest depths and glimpses the highest heights, swells with harmony and ascends in the creative mystery of melody, finds satisfaction and release in emotion and is one with the joy of the universe: it becomes a passion for beauty.

If we recognize that humanity is gradually nearing the third period of its destiny, we shall understand that the task of racial fusion will be accomplished on the Ibero-American continent in keeping with a law derived from the exercise of our highest faculties. The laws of emotion, beauty, and joy will govern the choice of partners, with results infinitely superior to those of a eugenics based on scientific reason and attentive only to the least important aspect of the act of love. The mysterious eugenics of aesthetic taste will prevail over the eugenics of science. Where radiant passion rules, restraints are unnecessary. The very ugly will not procreate, will not want to procreate; what will it matter, then, that all races will blend into one, if ugliness will find no cradle? Poverty, deficient education, the scarcity of beautiful individuals, the wretchedness that makes people ugly—all these calamities will vanish in the future stage of society. Then it will seem repulsive and criminal for a mediocre couple to boast, as is now common, of having multiplied misery. Marriage will cease to be a consolation for misfortunes that there is no reason to perpetuate and will become a work of art.

With the spread of education and prosperity, the danger of mixing radically opposite types will vanish. Unions will take place in keeping with the unique law of the third period, the law of mutual attraction, refined by the sense of beauty—a genuine attraction and not the false one imposed on us now by necessity and ignorance. These unions, sincerely passionate and easily dissolved in case of error, will produce bright and beautiful offspring. The whole species will change its physical appearance and its temperament; the higher instincts will prevail, and the elements of beauty that are now scattered among the various peoples will be fixed in a happy synthesis.

At present, in part out of hypocrisy and in part because such unions are formed between wretched persons in unfortunate circumstances, we are profoundly horrified by the marriage of a black woman to a white man. We should feel no repugnance whatsoever at the union of a black Apollo with a blond Venus, which proves that beauty sanctifies everything. On the other hand, it is repulsive to see those couples that every day issue from the courthouse or the church, about 90 percent of them ugly. Thanks to our vices, our prejudices, and our misery, the world is thus filled with ugliness. Procreation motivated by love is a good harbinger of choice offspring; but love must itself be a work of art, and not the refuge of despair. If what is to be passed on is stupidity, then what links the parents is not love, but a low and disreputable instinct.

A mixture of races consummated in keeping with the laws of social benefit, mutual attraction, and beauty will lead to the formation of a human type infinitely superior to all previous ones. By the Mendelian law of heredity, the crossbreeding of opposites will produce widely diverse and extremely complex variants, just as the human elements to be crossed are manifold and diverse; but precisely this assures us of the boundless possibilities that a well-directed instinct opens for the gradual perfection of our species.[15] If heretofore it has not improved much, that is because it has lived in crowded and miserable conditions that have impeded the functioning of the free instinct of beauty; reproduction has occurred after the fashion of beasts, with no quantitative limit and no aspiration toward improvement. The spirit has taken no part in it, only the appetite, which seeks satisfaction as best it can, so that at this point we cannot even imagine the modalities and effects of a series of truly inspired crossings. Unions based on talents and beauty ought to produce many individuals endowed with the dominant qualities. If we then choose, not with our reason but our taste, the qualities that we wish to prevail, the select individuals will become ever-more numerous, while the throwbacks will tend to disappear. Recessive offspring will no longer unite with

15. Mendelism, a series of genetic tenants derived from Austrian scientist and priest Gregor Johann Mendel (1822–1884), related to the transmission of hereditary characteristics from organisms to their offspring.

each other but will go in search of rapid improvement or will voluntarily suppress all desire for physical reproduction. The very conscience of the species will develop a shrewd Mendelism once it is freed from physical pressures, ignorance, and poverty; and thus monstrosities will vanish within very few generations, and what is normal today will come to seem abominable. The lower types of the species will be absorbed by the higher. The blacks, for example, could be redeemed in this fashion; and by means of voluntary extinction the ugliest breeds will gradually give way to the most beautiful. As the inferior races become educated, they will become less prolific, and the best specimens will gradually ascend on a scale of ethnic betterment, whose highest point is not exactly the white man, but that new race to which the white, too, will have to aspire in order to achieve synthesis. The Indian, by being grafted onto the kindred race, will leap across the thousands of years that separate Atlantis from our time; and within a few decades of aesthetic eugenics the black might disappear, along with such types as the free instinct for beauty might mark as fundamentally recessive and therefore unworthy of perpetuation. A process of selection through taste would thus prevail, one far more efficient than the brutal Darwinian selection that might be valid for inferior species, but never for man.

No race of our time can present itself as a perfect model to be imitated by all the others. The *mestizo* and the Indian, and even the black, surpass the white in countless genuinely spiritual abilities. Neither in antiquity nor today have we ever seen a race able to create a civilization on its own. Humanity's most illustrious epochs have been precisely those in which dissimilar people have come into contact and mixed. India, Greece, Alexandria, Rome, are so many examples of the fact that only geographical

and ethnic universality can yield the fruits of civilization. In the contemporary period, when the pride of the
current masters of the world, through the mouths of their
scientists, affirms the ethnic and mental superiority of the
white man of the North, any teacher can observe that the
children and young people in North American universities, descendants of Scandinavians, Dutch, and English,
are much slower, almost obtuse, in comparison with the
mestizo children and youth of the South. Perhaps this
superiority can be explained as the effect of a salutary
blending of opposite elements, a spiritual genetics. The fact
is that new blood renews vigor and that even the soul seeks
something different with which to enrich the monotony of
its contents. Only a long-term experiment will be able
to show the results of a mixture carried out not through
violence or out of necessity, but through choices arising
from bedazzlement with beauty and confirmed by the
emotional power of love.

In the first and second periods we are living in, the
human species, because of isolation and wars, is in a sense
living in conformity with Darwinian laws. The English,
who see nothing but the present of the external world,
did not hesitate to apply zoological theories to the field of
human sociology. If this incorrect application of a physi-
ological law to the realm of the spirit were acceptable,
then speaking of the ethnic absorption of the black would
amount to a defense of retrogression. Implicitly or openly,
the English theory presupposes that the black is a kind
of link closer to the ape than to the blond man. There
is consequently no option other than making him disappear. The white man, on the other hand, especially the
English-speaking white man, is presented as the sublime
culmination of human evolution; crossing him with
another race would mean befouling his stock.

Such a view of things, however, is nothing but the illusion cherished by every successful people during the time of its hegemony. Each of the great peoples of history has deemed itself the last and the chosen. When we compare these childish instances of pride one with another, we see that the mission that each people assigns to itself is at bottom nothing but lust for booty and the desire to exterminate its rival. Even official science is, in each period, a reflection of the pride of the dominant race. The Hebrews based their belief in their superiority on oracles and divine promises. The English base theirs on observations concerning domestic animals. Out of the observation of crossings and hereditary varieties of these animals grew Darwinism, first as a modest zoological theory, then as a social biology that assigns the Englishman absolute superiority over all other races. Every imperialism has need of a philosophy to justify it. The Roman Empire preached order, that is, hierarchy: first the Roman, then his allies, and slavery for the barbarian. The British preach natural selection, with the implied conclusion that by natural and divine right the world belongs to the dolichocephalic inhabitants of their islands and to their descendants. This science that came to invade us along with the products of conquering commerce can, however, be fought in the same way that every imperialism is fought, by opposing to it a superior science, a broader and more vigorous civilization. The fact is that no race is sufficient unto itself and that Humanity would be—indeed, is—the loser every time that a race disappears by violent means. It is all very well for each race to evolve as it chooses, but always within its own vision of beauty and without interrupting the harmonic development of human elements.

Each thriving race needs to create its own philosophy, the wellspring of its success. We have been educated under the humiliating influence of a philosophy devised by our enemies, sincerely perhaps, but with the aim of exalting their own purposes and crushing ours. Thus we have ourselves come to believe in the inferiority of the *mestizo*, in the hopelessness of the Indian, in the condemnation of the black, in the irremediable decadence of the Oriental. The rebellion of our arms was not followed by the rebellion of consciousness. We rebelled against the political power of Spain and did not notice that, along with Spain, we fell under the economic and spiritual domination of the race that has been mistress of the world since Spain's greatness came to an end. We shook off one yoke only to fall under another. We became victims of a shift in the locus of power that would have been inevitable even had we understood it in time. There is an inevitability in the destiny of peoples, just as in that of individuals, but now that a new phase of History is beginning it becomes necessary to reconstruct our ideology and organize every aspect of the life of our continent in keeping with a new ethnic doctrine. Let us then begin to live our own lives and make our own science. If we do not first free the spirit, we shall never succeed in redeeming the flesh.

———

Our obligation is to formulate the bases of a new civilization, and for that very reason we must bear in mind that neither in form nor in substance do civilizations repeat themselves. The theory of ethnic superiority has merely been a weapon employed by every warlike people, but the combat that faces us is so important that it allows of no such specious ruse. We do not maintain that we are or will become the world's leading race, the most enlightened, the strongest and most beautiful. Our aim is

even higher and more difficult to achieve than a transient
superiority. Our values exist in potentiality, so much so
that we are as yet nothing. Nonetheless, for the proud
Egyptians the Hebrew race was nothing but a vile breed
of slaves, and from it was born Jesus Christ, founder of
the greatest movement in History, proclaiming love for all
men. This love will be one of the fundamental dogmas of
the fifth race that will arise in America. Christianity liber-
ates and engenders life, because it contains a universal, not
national, revelation, which is why the Jews, who could
not bring themselves to join with Gentiles, had to reject
it. America, however, is the homeland of the Gentiles,
the true promised land of Christians. If our race proves
unworthy of this sacred soil, if it comes to lack love, it
will be replaced by peoples more qualified to carry out the
predestined mission of these lands, the mission of serving
as the home of a humanity made up of every nation and
every breed. The form of life that the progress of the world
forces on Hispanic America is not a rival creed that in
the face of its adversary says, "I shall overcome you or
do without you," but an infinite yearning for integration
and wholeness that necessarily invokes the universe. The
boundlessness of its desire guarantees it strength to fight
the exclusivistic creed of the enemy and confidence in the
victory that must always fall to the Gentiles. The danger
lies rather in our undergoing the same fate as the majority
of the Hebrews, whose refusal to become Gentiles lost
them the grace that had arisen among them. This is what
will happen to us if we prove incapable of offering home
and brotherhood to all men. Then another people will be
the axis, some other language will be the vehicle; but no
one can any longer hold back the fusion of peoples, the
coming of the fifth era of the world, the era of universality
and cosmic consciousness.

The doctrine of sociological and biological formation that we expound here is not simply an ideological effort to lift the spirits of a depressed race by offering it a thesis that contradicts the doctrine with which its rivals have tried to hold it down. The truth is that as the falseness of the scientific premise on which the dominance of today's world powers rests becomes more evident, we also come to glimpse, in experimental science itself, indications of a road that leads not to the triumph of one single race but to the redemption of all men. It is as though the palingenesis already proclaimed by Christianity thousands of years ago were now confirmed in the various branches of scientific knowledge. Christianity preached love as the basis of human relations, and we now begin to see that only love is capable of producing a superior Humanity. The policies of states and the science of the positivists, directly influenced by those policies, declared that not love was the law, but antagonism, struggle, and the survival of the fittest, with no criterion for judging fitness other than the curious *petitio principii* contained in the thesis itself, since he who survives is fit, and only the fit survives. Thus all the petty knowledge that tried to ignore sublime revelations and replace them with generalizations based on a mere sum of details is ultimately reduced to flawed verbal formulas of this sort.

———

The discredit into which such doctrines have fallen is augmented by the discoveries and observations that are revolutionizing the sciences today. It was impossible to assail the view of History as a series of frivolities as long as it was thought that individual life, too, lacked a metaphysical goal and a providential plan. But if mathematics is wavering and reshaping its conclusions to give us the concept of an unstable world whose mystery changes in keeping with our relative position and the nature of our concepts; if physics and chemistry no longer dare to affirm that in the processes of the atom there is nothing but the action of masses and forces; if biology, too—with Uexküll, for example— declares in its new hypotheses that in the course of life "cells move as though operating within a finished organism whose organs exist in a deliberate harmony and function together, that is, according to a plan," and that "there is a meshing of animate factors in the physico-chemical drive wheel" (which gainsays Darwinism, at least in the interpretation of those Darwinists who deny that Nature obeys a plan); if genetics also demonstrates, as Uexküll says, that protoplasm is a mixture of substances out of which more or less anything can be made; then, in the face of all these conceptual changes in science, we must recognize that the theoretical edifice supporting the domination of a single race has also collapsed.[16] This, in turn, also augurs the imminent collapse of the material power of those who have created all this false bargain science of conquest.

Mendel's Law, especially when it confirms the "participation of animate factors in the physico-chemical drive wheel," must form part of our new patriotism, for its terms lead to the conclusion that the different faculties of the spirit take part in the processes of destiny.

What does it matter that Spencerian materialism held us in subjection if we can now consider ourselves a kind of reserve for humanity, a promise of a future that will outstrip every earlier time? We are, then, in one of those

---

16. Jakob Johann von Uexküll (1864–1944), German biologist, a pioneer in the fields of muscular physiology, animal behavior studies, and cybernetics.

epochs of palingenesis and in the center of the universal maelstrom, and we must arouse all our faculties so that, active and alert, they may immediately take part in the processes of collective redemption. The dawn of a unique time is breaking. It is as though Christianity were to achieve consummation, but now not only in souls but in the very roots of men. As the instrument of this transcendental transformation, a race has been taking form in Ibero-America, full of vices and defects but endowed with malleability, a quick understanding, and ready emotions, which are fertile elements for the plasma that will create the future species. There is already an abundant supply of biological materials, characters, and the genes of which geneticists speak; only the organizing impulse has been lacking, the formative plan for the new species. What should characterize this creative impulse?

Were we to act in accordance with the first period's law of chaotic pure energy, in accordance with a rudimentary biological Darwinism, then blind force, almost mechanically imposing the most vigorous elements, would bring about simple and brutal decisions and exterminate the weak, or rather, those who do not fit in with the plan of the new race. By the very nature of the new order, however, the permanence of elements will not be based on violence but on taste, and selection will consequently be made spontaneously, in the manner of the painter who from among all colors chooses only those suitable for his work.

If we set about building the fifth race according to the law of the second period, a battle of wits would ensue in which the clever and unscrupulous would win out over the dreamers and the good-hearted. In that case the new humanity would probably be primarily Malay, as it is said that no one outdoes the Malays in wariness and astuteness and even, if necessary, in perfidiousness. The path of intelligence might even bring us, should we so desire, to a humanity of Stoics that accepted duty as the supreme norm. The world would become something like a vast Quaker village, where the plans of the spirit would eventually feel choked and deformed by rigid precept. For reason, pure reason, can recognize the benefits of the moral law but cannot endow action with the fighting zeal that makes it productive.

On the other hand, the true power to create joy is contained in the law of the third period, which is the emotion of beauty and a love so pure as to become indistinguishable from divine revelation. Since ancient times, for example in *Phaedrus*, love has been deemed to have the quality of pathos: its dynamism touches and moves our souls, transforms things and destiny itself. The race best able to sense this law and impose it on life and on things will be the matrix of the new era of civilization. Fortunately the *mestizos* of the Ibero-American continent, a people for whom beauty is the supreme justification of all things, possess this gift, necessary for the fifth race, to a high degree. Keen aesthetic sensibility and profoundly beautiful love, heedless of base self-interest and unfettered by formalism, are both necessary for the third period, impregnated with a Christian aestheticism that touches even ugliness itself with a redeeming pity that makes a halo to glow around all creation.

We have, thus, on our continent all the elements for the new humanity, a law that will select the factors for the creation of the predominant types and that will not be guided by national criteria, as a single conquering race would have to be, but by criteria of universality and beauty, and we also have the space and the natural resources. No European people, no matter how well endowed, could replace the people of Ibero-America in this mission, for each of those peoples has an already constituted culture and a tradition that is a hindrance in tasks of this kind. No conquering race could replace us, because it would necessarily impose its own characteristics, even if only out of the need to exercise violence to maintain its conquest. Neither can the peoples of Asia fulfill this universal mission; they are worn out, or at least lack the boldness for new undertakings.

The people that Hispanic America is now forming, as yet somewhat amorphous but possessed of a free and eager spirit because of our unexplored expanses, can still repeat the great deeds of the Spanish and Portuguese conquerors. The Hispanic race in general is still fated to undertake this mission of discovering new zones of the spirit, now that all lands have been explored. Only the Iberian part of America is endowed with the spiritual factors, the race, and the territory that are necessary for the great task of beginning the universal era of mankind. It contains all the races that will be making their contributions: the Nordic man, who is today the master of action but who had humble beginnings and seemed inferior at a time when several great cultures had already appeared and decayed; the black, as a reserve of possibilities that originate in the remote days of Lemuria; the Indian, who saw the end of Atlantis but whose consciousness contains a silent mystery. We have all the peoples and all the talents, and all that is needed is for genuine love to organize and activate the law of History.

Many obstacles stand in the way of the plan of the spirit, but they are obstacles that progress always faces. An immediate objection might be to ask how the different races will join in harmony when not even the children of a single stock can live in peace and joy within the economic and social system that now oppresses mankind. But this state of mind will have to change quickly. All the trends of the future are currently interrelated: Mendelism in biology, socialism in government, a growing openness in souls, general progress, and the appearance of the fifth race that will fill the planet with the triumphs of the first truly universal, truly cosmic culture.

If we take a broad view of the process, we shall see the three stages of society, each animated by the contributions of the four basic races that consummate their mission and then disappear in order to create a superior fifth ethnic type, so that we have five races and three stages, making the sum of eight, the number that in Pythagorean lore symbolizes the ideal of the equality of all men. Such coincidences or discoveries surprise us when first we come on them, though they might later seem trivial.

A few years ago, when the ideas that I am now attempting to present in rapid synthesis were as yet ill defined, I tried to express them symbolically through the new Palace of Public Education in Mexico. Lacking the means to do exactly what I wanted, I had to settle for a Spanish Renaissance building with two courtyards, arcades, and passageways that create an impression somewhat like a wing. For the panels at the four corners of the outer courtyard I commissioned allegories of Spain, Mexico, Greece, and India, the four civilizations that have the most to contribute to the formation of Latin America. Below these four allegories were to stand four great stone statues of the four great races of our time—the white, the red, the black, and the yellow—to indicate that America is home to all and needs them all. Finally, a monument was to be built in the center, in some manner symbolizing the law of the three stages: the material, the intellectual, and the aesthetic. In conjunction, all of this was to indicate that by means of the threefold law, we in America, before any other part of the globe, shall achieve the creation of a race composed of the treasures of all earlier races: the ultimate race, the cosmic race.

First published as preface to *La raza cósmica* (Barcelona: Agencia Mundial de Librería, 1925); the essay was repositioned as chapter 1 in the revised edition (Mexico City: Espasa-Calpe, 1948), and a prologue was added to the book.

The Race

Problem in

Latin

America

José Vasconcelos

Many theories have been advanced as to the origin of the old inhabitants of this New World. The discoveries of Professor Hrdlička, relating to strong similarities between a certain Siberian tribe and the North American red Indian, may be entirely correct, but they do not exclude the possibility of the existence of some more autochthonous stock coming from the very far south, from Patagonia, as the Peruvian legends seem to indicate.[1] Certain similarities that have often been

---

1. Aleš Hrdlička (1869–1943), U.S.-based Czech anthropologist who developed the theory of human colonization of the American continent from East Asia. His findings were used to document the theory of the global origin of the human species.

pointed out between the Maya Quiché architecture and the Egyptian manner of building would tend to confirm the opinion of the believers in the Atlantis of the classic days; and finally, the theory of Professor Wegener regarding the original unity of all continents in one body that has been separated as a result of the earth's rotation would clear away all sorts of difficulties, for it would allow us to state that there is no more mystery surrounding the whole of the human race. Farther back than five thousand years we do not know how we lived, nor where.

We can, however, assert that in the New World, just the same as in the Old, a series of civilizations have developed and decayed. Civilizations come and go, but it is very probable that the human stock, the particular race that creates a certain period of cultures, does not disappear with the disappearance of its constructive power. The social development of a certain people may stop entirely while the race itself goes on reproducing its members. The Greeks of the Roman days had disappeared as a ruling type of civilization but continued to exist as a race and traveled and mixed with other races; and the original stock thus became modified but never totally destroyed. The same thing can be said, I am sure, of the Indian. When Cortés arrived on the continent, the Indians of Montezuma did not themselves know who had been the builders of the Teotihuacan pyramids that were lying covered with the dust of centuries a few miles away from the old Tenochtitlán—the Mexico City of today. But there is no doubt that a great number of these Montezuma Indians had in their veins the same blood of the builders of the forgotten monuments. The Aztecs, who were comparative newcomers, may not have had it, but the strata of the older races inhabiting the valley were no doubt inheritors of the flesh and the soul of the high-type ancestors. The invaders never succeeded in destroying all of the subjected population, but had to coexist with them and naturally intermarried and learned from the older inhabitants. In the same manner we can affirm that, although the natives of Yucatan and Guatemala had forgotten all about the history of the builders of the Maya Quiché palaces, they still have in them the soul of the ancient architects. It is absolutely no wonder that a historical tradition should get lost in a time in which there was no written language; and even such written characters as existed were transmitted only through verbal tradition, with consequent danger of a total loss of the key to the symbols through periods of war, emigrations, and calamities.

The fact I am trying to emphasize then is that our race, the Indian races of the tropics at least, do not constitute a primitive stock. Call it, if you will, a decaying stock, but not a primitive stock. The new Mexico Indian may be primitive, although I would rather say that instead of being primitive he is provincial; that is to say, that what remains of his culture is derived from the little he could obtain, placed at such a distance from the higher civilizations of the southern sections of Guatemala and Mexico. I maintain that the spread of civilization at the time, as well as in the time of the Spaniards and way up into the seventeenth century, the spread of civilization in the New World was, and had been, from south to north instead of being as it is today and as it has been since the Declaration of American Independence, from north to south. Since the beginning of the nineteenth century, the Latin American countries began to take from the United States their political institutions, their school systems; and later we have taken the railroads, the machinery, and finally the capital for the development of our resources; but in the preceding centuries, during the day of the Indian and during the day of the Spaniards, it was the native of Arizona who had to march down to the south in search of tools for his wool-weaving and in search of inspiration for the drawings that decorated it. In the time of the Spaniard, the mission and the tillage both came from the better architecture and from the more advanced agriculture of Central Mexico, then the mother of Latin American culture. In South America we find a similar, though inverted, movement. There civilization was centered in the semitropics and the temperate plateau of Cuzco and scarcely reached the deserted plains of what is today the great, growing Argentinean nation. But the Aztec and the Inca sections were at that time not only the most densely populated but also the centers of the culture of the New World, the creators of civilization of that period.

Our Indians then are not primitive as was the red Indian, but old, century-tried souls who have known victory and defeat, life and death, and all of the moods of history.

I wish to call your attention to the fact that the Indians of Mexico as well as the Indians of Peru represented a certain type of civilization and consequently were not, as were the North American Indians, simply tribes of natives, wandering tribes of hunters, because this in itself perhaps explains why the Spaniard had to mix with the Indian, whereas the Englishman did not mix but simply forced the Indian back. Whenever two civilizations meet, one or the other becomes predominant, but they both undergo a change; they both lose certain traits and win others. What had happened to the Spaniard during the Arab invasion happened to the Indian during the Spanish invasion. There is a difference of course in degree, and, as we shall see later, a very surprising difference in results; but the truth is that the social, the historical process of the Spanish conquest in Mexico was about the same as any of the Asiatic or European invasions in which one race obtained control and predominance and the other was subjected, but after which both continued to live in close contact, modifying each other through that contact.

The case of North America, as we all know, was very different. This was not an invasion, at least not a sudden overwhelming invasion, but a long penetration of the territory without conservation of the native stock, and consequently without social contact or any other relation with the Indian.

This difference is the origin of the policy and of the practice of what we may call the one-race standard as against the mixed-race standard. By that I mean this undeniable fact that the civilization of North America is a one-race civilization, a white-race civilization as you insist on calling yourselves, sometimes even to the exclusion of other whites, such as, for instance, the Spaniard. A white civilization that may contain, and does contain, millions of other racial stocks, such as the Negro, but does not consider such dissimilar stock as a part of itself and does not as a rule intermarry with it. The Negro here, as well as the Indian, is in a world apart socially and is a body that is connected only politically with the white population. Of course nobody can deny the deep influence, and a gradually increasing influence, of the Negro upon the American mind—an influence that gives you the music to which you dance, and the laughter that helps your happiness, two heavenly gifts, lavishly spread by the socially isolated Negro.

On the other hand we have, in the south, a civilization that from the beginning accepted a mixed standard of social arrangement not only as a matter of fact but through law, because the Indian after being baptized became the equal of the Spaniard and was able to intermarry with the conqueror. The wedding of Cortés—who is accused of having murdered his Spanish wife in order to marry, or at least to live undisturbed with, his Indian love, La Malintzin—is symbolic of the new state of affairs and of the whole of the race situation in our country.[2] The example of Cortés in taking an Indian woman for his wife was followed by many others; it went on then and has been going on since; but the first time that the world realized what had happened in America was, I believe, when the first writer of the new race appeared in Peru. About the middle of the sixteenth century the learned public of Spain began to read with curiosity and amazement the works of the celebrated *mestizo*, surnamed El Inca—El Inca Garcilaso de la Vega, a historian, a man of letters, perhaps the first man of letters of the New World.[3] The writings of El Inca—very entertaining and fascinating reading even today—dealt with childhood memories of the life of his mother, an Indian princess, and his father, a Spanish captain. El Inca also wrote some tales and narratives about the conquest and about the feelings of the defeated natives; he heard and repeated in his writings many old stories taken from the lips of cacique ancestors; he impregnated himself with all the legend and all the sentiment of the dying Indian civilization; and then, while still a young man, he traveled through Spain and learned and adopted Spanish ideas and also learned to love Spain and Spanish European culture. His mind, as his own blood, became then the hyphen, the meeting point of the

---

2. La Malintzin, aka La Malinche, Malinalli, and Doña Marina (ca. 1496 or 1505–ca. 1529, and some sources give 1550–1551), Nahua woman who was Hernán Cortés's mistress and served as his translator.

3. "El Inca" Garcilaso de la Vega (1539–1616), Peruvian historian, author of *The Florida of the Inca* and *Royal Commentaries of the Incas*.

Spanish-Indian tragedy, all of which through his genius he succeeded in transforming into a new, broader concept of life. And it can be fairly said that in the days of Garcilaso there was no greater mind in this New World, either among the Indians or among the Spaniards, than the mind of this half-breed, who was struggling to make one mind of the two conflicting mentalities of the New World. And with Garcilaso the spiritual alliance of, the spiritual blending of, the Indian and the Spaniard was sealed forever.

Since then, more and more every day, the fortunes of the Spanish American countries have been passing into the hands of men who acknowledge Garcilaso as their spiritual ancestors. We have been at the heart Spaniards even when we have had to fight against Spain, and we remain Indians even when our skin accidentally becomes whitened through marriage with the more recent Spanish stock. In this way the half-breed cannot entirely go back to his parents because he is not exactly as any of his ancestors; and being unable to connect fully with the past, the *mestizo* is always directed toward the future—is a bridge to the future. No country can show, better than Mexico can, all of the signs and the effects of this particular *mestizo* psychology.

Notice the fact that the *mestizo* represents an entirely new element in history; for if it is true that in all times the conquered and the conqueror have mixed their bloods, it is also unquestionably true that never before had there come together and combined two races as wide apart as the Indian and the Spanish, and never before had the fusing processes of two such different castes been made on such a large scale. History had never witnessed this process of two unrelated breeds intermingling and practically disappearing in order to create a new one. According to some observers, all of our backwardness, all of our difficulties and unfruitful struggles are derived from the fact of this unsound and even contemptible mixture of races. A noted philosopher, who for a time was the master even of our own *mestizo* universities, the Englishman Spencer, specifically pointed to us as an example of a hopeless hybrid product of the violation of the sacred scientific rules of a purifying, uplifting evolution. At any rate, the English have always stood for the conservation of an original unmixed human stock and have succeeded in maintaining it; and the Spaniards have always disregarded this purely white prejudice and have actually created the millions of the *mestizo* stock of America and of the Philippines. The unlimited progress of the Anglo-Saxons in civilization in the late centuries has led to the belief in the soundness of their policy. Many even among ourselves felt as though we had to admit that racial hybridism could only produce a low type of humanity, an inferior stock that could only be aided by the constant increase of a renewed wave of white people such as has flooded, for instance, the unpopulated territories of Argentina. Such is still the belief of some Latin Americans of the purer European stock; and there are many *mestizos* who feel that all of their reproductive efforts should favor the elimination of the native strain.

To me this late attitude is nothing but a case of cowardice. We are dazzled by the power of the world's civilization at the present moment, and we forget that there is in hybridism something deeper than can be observed by the superficial thinker. It is very easy to agree with success; it is very easy to philosophize with the partial conclusions of a given moment of history. But if we think with our heads and if we search with our own souls into the mysteries of human destiny, we immediately find that the so-called pure-race theory is nothing but the theory of the dominating people of every period of history. And the pure-race theory leads, very often almost fatally, to parentally arranged marriages, to the incestuous marriages of the Pharaohs. If we observe human nature closely, we find that hybridism in man, as well as in plants, tends to produce better types and tends to rejuvenate those types that have become static. If we go through history, we find that after a period of adaptation the results of the renewal of blood are always beneficial. Even some of the most modern authors on the subject, such as the Frenchman Pittard, conclude that a pure race is a myth because all nations are the result of numerous mixtures; he goes further and states that "it is only the poor devils" that can claim a unmixed pedigree, because only the lower classes among has-been nations marry between themselves, while the powerful of any group always enrich their experience by marrying some of the prettiest or more attractive women of the neighboring tribe.[4] The advantages of a mixture of races has then been generally recognized; race prejudice as it exists today is a comparatively modern feeling and originates perhaps from the necessity of the English colonizer of far-distant territories densely populated by dissimilar races. The Englishman with his highly developed social instinct understood that if his colonizers of the distant territory of the Indies began to marry the native women, very soon the European in them would become absorbed, and the next generation would become lost for the Empire. The Spaniards were bolder; for the decision to accept the results of intermarrying the native was not without forethought, but perfectly calculated, as is shown by the long discussion that preceded the papal statement to the effect that the Indians were entitled to receive the sacraments of the church, marriage among them.

Now if we compare the results of the English policy in India with the results of the Spanish policy in America,

---

4. Eugène Pittard (1867–1962), French ethnographer, author of *Race and History: An Ethnological Introduction to History*.

even at the time when the British policy is not yet ripe, not having had the centuries of the Spanish colonization's experience, I believe that we shall be justified in declaring that the cultural results of the Spanish method are superior. The Spanish have succeeded in reproducing their blood in part and their culture in full in twenty nations that are today about as Spanish as Spain itself can be, though independent politically and socially. The English, on the other hand, with their system of not even maintaining social intercourse with the natives of India are today as completely strangers in India as on the day their ancestors first landed; and it does not seem probable that they will ever succeed in eradicating the Indian, to substitute for him the Islander. We find in India a coexistence, a juxtaposition, of cultures that do not mix, in the same manner that the bodies of the two races remain fatally apart. Which system is ultimately the better, even from the selfish point of view of the conqueror, is something that only the future can answer. We do not pretend to give advice, but we are bound to accept the Spanish method, which in a way has created our nationalities and is the very reason of our existence as a race and a branch of the human family. We cannot condemn the Spanish method without denying ourselves.

The founders of the United States were fortunate in not finding in this territory a very large Indian population, and so it was easy for them to push the Indian back; but the importation of the Negro has brought to this nation, as we all know, a problem harder, no doubt, than any known before. And the North Americans, who are the result of a mixture of all the European races, have followed the English system in regard to the Negro, that is to say, the system of strict avoidance of matrimonial relations with the colored race. The Spaniards did not obey this rule of abstention even with the Negro; the population of many of our tropical sections is largely mulatto, a mixture of the Spanish and the Negro. The Portuguese have also created a mulatto population in Brazil; so here again, we find the Latin system of assimilation and intermarriage and mixture opposed to the Anglo-Saxon method of matrimonial taboos and pure-race standards.

If the tremendous problem involved in this coexistence of two races that live apart in the same home could be considered as finally solved in this country, then there would be a good argument for those who claim that Mexico should try to do away with the *mestizo* and the Indian population by importing millions of Europeans; but the fact is that you cannot destroy a race, that you cannot change social conditions at will, and that you have to face the problem not only with the brain but also with the heart and the superior instinct of nature. And at least for us in Mexico, it is too late to change our practices. There I nothing left for us to do but to follow the Spanish tradition of eliminating the prejudice of color, the prejudice of race in all of our social procedures. No matter what our theoretical opinions might be, we have to start from the fact that the *mestizo* is the predominating element in Mexico.

But the *mestizo* of Mexico does not hold an undisputed reign over the country. Once in a while you still hear in Mexico an echo of the Indian voice that clamors for the return to the past of the race as a means of obtaining strength and inspiration. The claims of the pure Indian sound sometimes almost as distinct in its vision as the creed of the most ardent advocate of the purity of the white in his own country. And the evidence that this is not merely a theoretical feeling is found in the story of our revolutions, which in some cases have developed purely Indian movements with the tendency to reinstate purely

Indian standards. The Indian uprisings in Yucatan, known as *guerra de castas*, the "war of castes," the pure Indian against the *mestizo* and the *criollo*, against the Spanish-speaking, against the Mexican population, is an old but clear example.[5] The Zapata movement of the last revolution clearly contained the seeds of an Indian revival over the whole extent of our country. There was a time when the European dress was not allowed in the Zapata territory; and those Mexicans of white Spanish skin that happened to join the Zapata armies had to adopt the dress and the manners of the Indian, in a certain way had to become *Indianized* before they could be accepted. But the weakness of the pure Indian movement lies of course in the fact that the Indian has no civilized standards upon which to fall back. He has no language of his own, never had a language common to all of the race. And the advantage of the Spanish method of colonization though assimilation is here again demonstrated, I believe, in the fact that the Spanish spirit is still gaining victories over the native Indian spirit through its language, its religion, and its social forms of living. Even the more radical leaders of the Zapata revolt, pure Indians like the schoolteacher Montaño who was the brains of the group, were expressing themselves in good Spanish and were basing their economic theory of the distribution of the land, et cetera, on the terms of the European manner of life.[6] At the same time, the masses of the rebelling Indians were carrying, as in the days of Hidalgo, the image of the Virgin of Guadalupe as a banner. They were being Spaniards even against their will

---

5. This uprising of Mayan Indians against the white and *mestizo* population in the southeastern Yucatán peninsula (1847–1901) caused approximately 250,000 deaths.

6. Otilio Montaño (1887–1917), schoolteacher and general under Emiliano Zapata's army, was instrumental in the drafting of the Plan of Ayala.

and their knowledge; and it is only natural that all of this should happen, as they had no other tradition upon which to fall back. On the other hand, the movement, although very conscientiously prepared, was overpowered by the stronger *mestizo* element of the armies of Carranza, of Obregón, and of Villa, who represented the Mexican rather than the Indian, that is to say, the Spanish American, the Indo-Spaniard, who also prevails in Central America, in Peru, and in Bolivia.[7]

You may ask if the *criollo*, the descendant of the pure Spanish blood, has not also tried to gain control of Mexico, and I believe we can answer that the *criollo* has made efforts to predominate and also has failed in such efforts. I believe that such tendencies as those represented by the group that aligned itself with Maximilian were mainly European, Spanish tendencies.[8] And to defeat them, the *mestizo* and the Indian joined under the leadership of the Indian Benito Juárez.[9] Since that time I am sure that the alliance between the *mestizo* and the Indian has become final, and of course, there being no dividing line by reason of color or caste, the *criollo* also has entirely adapted himself to a national sentiment, or rather to a continental sentiment of Ibero-Americanism, that has as a common

7. Venustiano Carranza (1859–1920), leader of the Mexican Revolution and president of Mexico, during whose term a version of the country's constitution was written. Álvaro Obregón (1880–1928), commander-in-chief of Mexico's revolutionary forces and president of Mexico from 1920 to 1924. Francisco "Pancho" Villa, pseudonym of José Doroteo Arango Arámbula (1878–1923), prominent general during the Mexican Revolution.

8. Maximiliano I of Mexico, aka Archduke Ferdinand Maximilian Joseph of Austria (1832–1867), a member of the Imperial House of Habsburg-Lorraine, proclaimed emperor of Mexico in 1864 during the Second Mexican Empire, with the backing of Napoleon III of France.

9. Benito Pablo Juárez García (1806–1872), Zapotec Indian and president of Mexico from 1858 to 1861, served as interim president from 1861 to 1865 and from 1865 to 1872.

indestructible bond the Spanish language and the Spanish type of culture.

The truth is then that whether we like it or not the *mestizo* is the dominant element in the Latin American continent. His characteristics have been pointed out many a time: a great vivacity of mind; quickness of understanding, and at the same time an unsteady temperament; not too much persistence in purpose; a somewhat defective will. It is curious to note that the blending of two different souls through inheritance has produced broader mental disposition. From a purely intellectual point of view I doubt whether there is a race with less prejudice, more ready to take almost any mental adventure, more subtle, and more varied than the *mestizo*, or half-breed. I find in these traits the hope that the *mestizo* will produce a civilization more universal in its tendency than any other race of the past. Whether it is owing to our temperament or to the fact that we do not possess a very strong national tradition, the truth is that our people are keen and are apt to understand and interpret the most contradictory human types. We feel the need of expressing life though many channels, through a thousand channels; we are not addicted to local tradition or to the European, but we desire to know and to try all—the East and the West, the North and the South. A plurality of emotion, an almost mad desire to try and to live life from every point of view and every manner of sense experience—we are perhaps more truly universal than any other people. Notwithstanding, we sometimes appear to be bigoted and patriotically local, but this is a result of the dangerous political position in which we have been placed in recent years. On the other hand we are unstable, and this I believe can be easily understood by the biologist, as we are a new product, a new breed, not yet entirely shaped. I believe such weakness can be overcome by obtaining a clear definition of our aim and by devoting ourselves to a definite and a great task.

Many of our failings arise from the fact that we do not know exactly what we want. First of all, then, we ought to define our own culture and our own purposes, and educate ourselves to them. No nation has ever risen to true greatness without an ardent faith in some high ideal. Democracy and equal opportunities for every man has been the motto of the great American nation. Broadness, universality of sentiment and thought, in order to fulfill the mission of bringing together all the races of the earth and with the purpose of creating a new type of civilization, is, I believe, the ideal that would give us in Latin America strength and vision.

The goal may seem too ambitious, but it is only great, unlimited ideals that are capable of giving a nation the strength that is required to break the routine of life and to outdo itself. The more ambitious the goal is, the more strenuous the effort becomes. Our mystic temperament demands a task that has, in itself at least, a tendency that is unbounded and almost impossible. A fiery impetus is our only hope if we are to catch up with the world. Our struggle is, in a way, the struggle of the future, because every day mankind will come more and more into contact, and mixtures of all sorts of blood and thought and sentiment will go on increasing, and with them the phenomena and the problems of *mestizaje* will become universal. The time and the opportunity of the one-blood, a pure-blood, group is passing away; everywhere the pure-blood groups are being absorbed; and even if they have been masters, they will not stand long before the increasing wave of the technically educated masses of the complex breed. In a way, the world is coming back to the confusion of Babel, and there may come a long period where mixture, what we call *mestizaje*, is bound to be the rule. We cannot then dispose of the problem by declaring, as the evolutionists of the Spencer school declared, that the hybrid type was a degenerate type. Such a statement represents only the shortsighted opinion of prejudice and the view advantageous to the imperialist. Let us remember, though, that all imperialisms have been swallowed exactly by those same masses they despised. The future will have to be prepared for in a different manner if we wish to see not a repetition of history but a new era in human progress.

From our local point of view in Mexico, I have started to preach the gospel of the *mestizo* by trying to impress on the minds of the new race a consciousness of their mission as builders of entirely new concepts of life. But if the mixed race is going to be able to do anything at all, it is first necessary to give it moral strength and faith in its own ability. The sort of science we have been teaching in our schools was not fit for this purpose; on the contrary it was the science created to justify the aims of the conqueror and the imperialist—the science that came to the help of the strong in their conquest and exploitation of the weak: the aristocracy of the white man and the empire of the white over the world, not only in the name of might but also on the ground of a certain semi-scientific theory of the survival and predominance of the fittest, which is popularly known as Nietzschean evolutionism, from Nietzsche, the German.[10] One of the first steps toward our moral regeneration, which I have been advocating in Mexico, is the abandonment of this blind belief in certain hasty deductions from Darwinism and the substitution of Mendelism for Darwinism in our biological philosophy,

---

10. Friedrich Wilhelm Nietzsche (1844–1900), German philosopher, author of *Human, All Too Human* and *Thus Spoke Zarathustra*, among other books.

as we might find more racial hope and more individual strength and faith in the Mendelian hypothesis of life. Modern scientific theories are in many cases like the religious creeds of the old days, simply the intellectual justification of fatalities of conquest and of commercial greed. If all nations then build theories to justify their policies or to strengthen their deeds, let us develop in Mexico our own theories; or at least, let us be certain that we choose among the foreign theories of thought those that stimulate our growth instead of those that restrain it. And so, instead of taking up, for instance, the Indian problem with the point of view of the ethnologist of the evolutionistic school who starts from the *parti pris* of his theory, according to which it will take the Indian about five thousand years to develop up to the mentality of the white, we ought to open our eyes to the fact that the Indian five thousand years ago was building monuments that the mentality of the white is using this very day as an inspiration for its new wonder cities of Chicago and New York. The racial theory to which we ought to subscribe then is the theory that the differences among peoples depend more upon the ability to do certain things to the exclusion of other things rather than to differences of degree in their total development. Some races chiefly develop artistic ability; other people develop commercial aptitude; and so on. The conclusion of this theory would then be extremely favorable to the *mestizo* type of culture, as it tends to complement the weaknesses of a particular stock through interchange and assimilation with all the world. In fact, all of the great periods of history have been the work of a mixture of races, of peoples and cultures, rather than the work of any privileged pure-blood nation.

The policy of segregation of the races and the policy of educating the Indian or any other race of our Latin

American countries according to separate standards of any sort, is not only absurd among us, but it would be fatal. It would be doubly fatal because we do not have that element of pure racial stock that could undertake in our land that supposed leadership that has been taken here by the New Englander. Even if it should be true that this unmixed white leadership has created the greatness of the United States, we do not have in Mexico anything equivalent to this root. Our progress may have been delayed on this account, but there is nothing left for us to do except to go ahead with the situation that nature has made for us; and instead of a blind, shortsighted copying of methods, we should go along creating what is required by our own problem and mission. For us, there is only one sound race policy, and that is the policy of old—the policy of the Spaniard and the Christian who took it for granted that we are all potentially the same and that we are bound to respond differently according to the call that is made upon us, each one bearing a treasure that comes to life at the proper moment in the time of need. The duty of any great culture is then to raise human beings as a whole and to call races together so that they can all collaborate in the task of a truly material and spiritual civilization. Do not put a man to a task for which he is not fitted. Place every one in his own vocation. Bring down to social practical life a little of the rule of joy instead of the hard, blind rules of need and of duty, and you will transform the world. But if we are ever going to approach any realization of this sort, we must start first by transforming all of our theories. For it is in the soul where the germ of our disease should be sought, in the mind, and more particularly in the heart. As long as our ideals do not correspond to our intimate wish and desire, our ideals will not be worthwhile. As long as pleasure and joy do not become the rule of life, we must admit that we are lost in a mistaken path. Duty is a means, knowledge is a means, effort is a means; joy and pleasure are the only ends. And there can be no joy in a civilization where races are separated by hatred, prejudice, and misunderstanding.

I have said that humanity is going back to Babel, and by this I mean that the day of the isolated civilization is over. In this new coming-together of all the races we ought not to repeat the methods of the past, the methods that transformed Babel into a curse. Babel became a curse because the different people did not understand each other and consequently, instead of concurring in a common purpose, they entered into competition and jealousy that destroyed every one of them. It is time then that we should change our methods in order to make the new period of Babel a prosperous one. The whole theory of the superiority of one stock above the other will have to be changed. The practice of putting the so-called lower races to work for the benefit of the superior will have to be abandoned or else the dominators will have to suffer from the revenge of the oppressed. This revenge is found in the law of nature itself. Notice the fact that whenever two extremely differentiated groups come into contact, it is, in the long run, the lower group that predominates if the superior does not undertake the task of raising the level of the inferior. The Spanish civilization is perduring today in America, not on account of the pure descendants of the conqueror but because of the mixed race and the Indian race that were educated and assimilated by the Spaniards. If the Spaniard had not mixed his blood with the Indian, there would not be today on the map a large area of countries where the Spanish soul is alive and progressive. When, on the contrary, the dominating race stands apart and takes no interest in the life of the inferior, the inferior tends instinctively to increase its numbers in order to compensate through numbers what the dominating race achieves through quality. The more civilized a nation is, the more it reduces its reproduction, the tendency being to obtain an advantage in quality. But the lower, opposed breed, having no control, no hope, goes on multiplying madly; and the weight and the curse of this overpopulation is just as harmful to the elect as it is to the less fortunate. If we are ever to stop this misery, it is necessary that the superior take pains to educate the inferior and to raise its standards. If we do not wish to be overwhelmed by the wave of the Negro, of the Indian, or of the Asiatic, we shall have to see that the Negro, the Indian, and the Asiatic are raised to higher standards of life, where reproduction becomes regulated and quality predominates over numbers. Instead of the competitive manner of life advocated by the defenders of pure-race civilization and by the imperialists and conquerors, we shall have to adopt then the cooperative, collaborating manner of interracial organization; instead of the struggle for life and the survival of the fittest, a collaboration of all human efforts for the production of a variety in quality—a salvation brought about, not through the elect of a certain type more or less strong, but through the utilization of every particular aptitude for the purpose of creating superior values. If the mad competition and distrust of the present day can be overcome, every race will then be able to work for the achievement of quality, and no race will devote itself to merely creating numbers; thereby the present-day danger of the overpowering of the superior few by the uncivilized many will disappear.

If we thus turn selfish competition into farsighted collaboration, it will not even matter much if we follow the pure-race, the one-race standard or the mixed-race standard. The very same differences of skin and temperament that today seem so distressing may become useful and even pleasing the moment that we learn to develop a task in which every special capacity finds its purpose and a reward. Spiritual affinities and similar fancies of taste and mind will then prevail, and a superior life will become the endeavor of the human family as a whole.

This is the third and final Norman Wait Harris Memorial Foundation lecture, delivered by José Vasconcelos at the University of Chicago in 1926. The general title of the three lectures was "The Latin American Basis of Mexican Civilization." Reprinted, with minor alterations, from José Vasconcelos and Manuel Gamio, *Aspects of Mexican Civilization* (Chicago: University of Chicago Press, 1926).

Chronology

1882: FEB. 28   José Vasconcelos is born in Oaxaca, the capital city of the Mexican state of the same name. His parents are Ignacio Vasconcelos and Carmen Calderón Conde.

1887   Moves with his family to Piedras Negras, on the U.S.-Mexican border, in the northern Mexican state of Coahuila.

1888   Enters an English-language primary school in Eagle Pass, Texas.

1895   Relocates with his family to Mexico City and briefly attends the Instituto de Toluca.

1896   Moves with his family to Campeche, in southeastern Mexico, and enters secondary school at the Instituto de Ciencias.

1898   Graduates from the Instituto de Ciencias, in Campeche.

1899   Enrolls at the Escuela Nacional Preparatoria in Mexico City. His family moves back to Piedras Negras, where his mother dies.

1901   Enters the Escuela de Jurisprudencia in Mexico City.

1905   Graduates with the thesis "Teoría

dinámica del derecho" (Dynamic Theory of Law). Works as a secretary and law clerk in Durango and Mexico City.

1906   In Tlaxcala, marries Serafina Miranda of Tlaxiaco, Oaxaca.

1907   Is admitted to the bar. Publishes *Teoría dinámica del derecho.*

1908: OCT. 28   Along with some friends, founds the anti–Porfirio Díaz literary salon, Ateneo de la Juventud.

1909: APR. 25   Formally joins the anti-Díaz Partido Nacional Antireeleccionista in Mexico City. Is named one of its secretaries and becomes the codirector of its weekly periodical, *El Antireeleccionista,* soon suppressed by Díaz.

1910   Publishes the anti-Díaz book *Gabino Barreda y las ideas contemporáneas* (Gabino Barreda and Contemporary Ideas), resulting in Díaz's order for his arrest. Escapes to New York, returning to Mexico City after three months.

1910: OCT. 5   Backs Francisco I. Madero's "Plan of San Luis Potosí."

1911   Pursued in Mexico City by Díaz's police. Closes his law office and relocates to Washington, D.C., where he is authorized to continue working for Madero.

1911: JULY   Upon Díaz's resignation and Madero's triumph, returns to Mexico City and reopens his office. Is named president of the Ateneo de la Juventud.

1911: SEPT. 2   The name of the Partido Nacional Anti-reeleccionista is changed by Madero to

	the Partido Constitucional Progresista and Vasconcelos is made vice president of its executive committee.
1911: NOV. 6	Madero assumes the presidency of the Mexican republic.
1912: OCT.	Rebellion led by Félix Díaz breaks out, with clandestine support from Victoriano Huerta, supposedly Madero's supporter.
1913: JAN.	Vasconcelos futilely warns Madero in person against Huerta.
1913: FEB. 18	Huerta is named the country's president.
1913: FEB. 22	Madero is assassinated.
1913: MAR. 26	Venustiano Carranza issues the "Plan of Guadalupe," repudiating Huerta. Vasconcelos is sent to London and Paris as Carranza's confidential agent.
1914	Named director of Escuela Nacional Preparatoria by Carranza.
1914: OCT. 8	Refusing to support Carranza unconditionally, Vasconcelos resigns directorship of the Escuela Nacional Preparatoria. Is jailed but escapes to Aguascalientes.
1914: NOV.	A political convention in Aguascalientes names General Eulalio Gutiérrez Mexico's interim president. In turn, Gutiérrez names Vasconcelos minister of public instruction.
1915: JAN. 16	Gutiérrez and Vasconcelos escape from Villistas in Mexico City.
1915: JAN. 20	Gutiérrez, declared no longer provisional president, escapes to the United States.
1915: APR.	Gutiérrez sends Vasconcelos to Washington, D.C., as his representative. Vasconcelos subsequently resigns.

1915: OCT.	The United States officially recognizes Carranza's government in Mexico.
1915: NOV.	Vasconcelos withdraws from public life.
1916	Publishes *Pitágoras: Una teoría del ritmo* (Pythagoras: A Theory of Rhythm), *Prometeo vencedor* (A Winning Prometheus), and *La intelectualidad mexicana* (The Mexican Intelligentsia). Accepts a post with the Escuelas Internacionales and leaves for South America.
1917	Leaves Escuelas Internacionales and returns to New York.
1918	Earns a living as a corporate lawyer across the United States. Publishes *El monismo estético* (Esthetic Monism).
1919	Abandons professional life and relocates to California.
1920	Publishes *Estudios indostánicos* (Indostanic Studies) and *La caída de Carranza: De la dictadura a la libertad* (The Fall of Carranza: From Dictatorship to Freedom).
1920: MAY 21	Carranza is killed in Mexico. Vasconcelos returns to Mexico City.
1920: JUNE 9	Adolfo de la Huerta, named provisional president of Mexico, appoints Vasconcelos as the first chancellor of Mexico's Universidad Nacional, eventually known as Universidad Nacional Autónoma de México (U.N.A.M.).
1920: JUNE 18	Vasconcelos begins a formal campaign against illiteracy.
1920: DEC. 1	Álvaro Obregón assumes the presidency and places national presses at the disposal of the Universidad Nacional. Vasconcelos begins a monthly journal, *El Maestro,*

	while he continues forming the Ministry of Education.
1921	Travels constantly around Mexico, promoting education.
1921: Feb. 9	Begins the publication of a series of classic titles in translation.
1921: Apr. 15	Starts a free breakfast program in Mexico's public schools.
1921: Apr. 27	Produces shield and motto for the Universidad Nacional: "Por mi raza hablará el espíritu" (My Spirit Shall Speak in Behalf of My Race). Also begins arranging for his elected successor.
1921: Sept. 20	Inaugurates the Primer Congreso Internacional de Estudiantes.
1921: Oct. 3	Announces the Acta Constitutiva de Federación de Intelectuales Latinoamericanos, serving as president of the steering committee.
1921: Oct. 12	Ceases to be chancellor of the Universidad Nacional and is immediately appointed secretary of education.
1922	Publishes *Divagaciones literarias* (Literary Variations), *Orientaciones del pensamiento en México* (Intellectual Paths in Mexico). Sets up libraries throughout Mexico and subsidizes the muralist movement of Diego Rivera, José Clemente Orozco, and David Alfaro Siqueiros. Patronizes national folk arts, founds a national symphony, and carries out the first census of indigenous regions and languages. Is also designated a special ambassador to South America.
1923	Establishes the beginnings of the National

Polytechnical Institute in Mexico City. Develops "cultural missions" in rural towns and is named Maestro de la Juventud by students of Colombia, Peru, and Panama.

1924   Publishes *Ideario de acción* (An Ideology for Action), *La revulsión de la energía: Los ciclos de la fuerza, el cambio y la existencia* (The Revulsion of Energy: The Cycles of Force, Change, and Existence). Resigns as secretary of education, accepting the candidacy for the governorship of the state of Oaxaca, where he is popularly elected. The central government refuses to recognize him in office, though. Begins collaborating with the newspaper *El Universal* and starts the periodical *La Antorcha.*

1925   Publishes *La raza cósmica* (The Cosmic Race), which includes the opening essay "Mestizaje." Leaves Mexico for Europe via Cuba. Travels to Spain, settling in Paris.

1926   Publishes *Indología: Una interpretación de la cultura iberoamericana* (Indology: An Interpretation of Ibero-American Culture), a sequel of sorts to *La raza cósmica.* Publishes the final issues of the periodical *La Antorcha* and travels by invitation to Central America. Also delivers three lectures sponsored by the Norman Wait Harris Foundation at the University of Chicago. The third is called "The Race Problem in Latin America."

1927   Travels throughout Europe.

1928	Lectures in universities across the United States, addressing political as well as academic topics. Accepts the nomination for president of Mexico from the Partido Constitucional Progresista.
1928: NOV. 10	Encouraged to return to public life, enters Mexico via the border town of Nogales. Runs as a candidate in Mexico's presidential election against Álvaro Obregón, who wins but is assassinated before he can take office for his second, nonconsecutive term.
1929	Publishes *Tratado de metafísica* (Metaphysical Treatise). Runs again for president, this time against Pascual Ortíz Rubio. Campaigns along Mexico's Pacific coast, then in the central and northern states.
1929: NOV. 17	The election is marred by controversy. Vasconcelos is opposed by both the U.S. and central Mexican governments and ends up being exiled to the United States after issuing in Nogales his "Plan of Guaymas," advocating a Mexican rebellion.
1930	Disillusioned with political efforts, leaves for Panama, where he lectures against U.S. imperialism and the Calles regime.
1931	Publishes *Ética* (Ethics) and *Pesimismo alegre* (Happy Pessimism). Goes to Paris.
1933	Moves to Argentina. Publishes *Sonata mágica: cuentos y relatos* (Magical Sonata: Stories and Narratives).
1934	Publishes *Bolivarismo y Monroismo:*

Temas iberoamericanos (Bolivarism and Monroism: Ibero-American Themes). In Chile, completes the first volume of his autobiographical memoirs, *Ulises criollo* (Creole Ulysses).

1935 Publishes *Estética* (Esthetics). Moves to New Orleans, then to San Antonio, Texas.

1936 Moves to Austin, Texas. Completes and publishes *La tormenta* (The Storm), second of four volumes of *Ulises criollo*.

1937 Publishes *Historia del pensamiento filosó-fico* (History of Philosophical Thought) and *Breve historia de México* (Brief History of Mexico).

1938 *El desastre* (The Disaster), the third volume of the memoirs, appears.

1939 Moves to Mexico City. Publishes *El proconsulado* (The Proconsulate), the fourth and final volume of his memoirs. The abbreviated English translation, under the title *A Mexican Ulysses*, appears under the aegis of Indiana University Press.

1940 Publishes *Manual de filosofía* (Philosophical Manual) and *Páginas escogidas* (Selected Pages).

1941 Publishes *Hernán Cortés: Creador de la nacionalidad* (Hernán Cortés: Creator of Our Nationality). Vasconcelos's first wife dies.

1943 Marries pianist Esperanza Cruz.

1945 Publishes *Lógica orgánica* (Organic Logic) and *El viento de Bagdad* (The Wind of Baghdad).

1946	Named director of Mexico's Biblioteca Nacional.
1952	Publishes *Filosofía estética* (Esthetic Philosophy).
1955	Publishes *Temas contemporáneas* (Contemporary Themes).
1957	Publishes *El ocaso de mi vida* (The Dusk of My Life).
1958	Elected vice president of the Federación Internacional de Sociedades Filosóficas. Releases *Don Evaristo Madero*.
1959: JUNE 30	Dies at his Mexico City home.

Acknowledgments

Gracias, first and foremost, to Adi Hovav, my editor at Rutgers University Press, for commissioning this book, and to Leslie Mitchner, editor in chief at the press, for shepherding it through the editorial process. Over the years, I have discussed José Vasconcelos's racial views in a number of a number of venues, including the *Chronicle of Higher Education*. My gratitude to my editor Karen Winkler for welcoming me to its pages. A number of people have been supportive at various stages: John R. H. Polt, who translated on my behalf Vasconcelos's essay "Mestizaje" in the late 1990s. His patience throughout the years, while I embarked on other projects, has been unremitting. My friend Héctor Vasconcelos, one of José Vasconcelos's children, whose diplomatic work in Boston allowed us to share enchanting discussions, was the first to suggest the idea that I write of a profile of his father. He pointed me in the direction of *Aspects of Mexican Civilization*, a volume of lectures by Vasconcelos and anthropologist Manuel Gamio, where "The Race Problem in Latin America" is featured.

Thanks, too, to Harold Augenbraum at the National Book Foundation; Anna Gillis of the National Endowment for the Humanities, who is an editor at *Humanities* magazine, where a portion of my profile "The Prophet of

Race" first appeared; Reed Malcolm at the University of California Press; Julia Reidhead and Kurt Wildermuth at W. W. Norton; and Elda Rotor at Penguin Classics. For the chronology of Vasconcelos and my profile, I made use the database of the Nettie Lee Benson Latin American Collection, housed in the University of Texas at Austin. I also found the following sources useful: Luis Villoro's *Los grandes momentos del indigenismo en México* (1950), John H. Haddox's *Vasconcelos of Mexico: Philosopher and Prophet* (1967); José Joaquín Blanco's *Se llamaba Vasconcelos: Una evocación crítica* (1977); Joaquín N. Cárdenas's *José Vasconcelos: Guía y profeta* (1985); Martha Robles's *Entre el poder y las letras: Vasconcelos en sus memorias* (1989); and Luis A. Marentes's *José Vasconcelos and the Writings of the Mexican Revolution* (2000).

About the Author

Ilan Stavans is the Lewis-Sebring Professor in Latin American and Latino Culture at Amherst College.

CPSIA information can be obtained at www.ICGtesting.com
Printed in the USA
270098BV00001B/9/P